This Business of Books
3rd Edition

"A Quick and Easy Read"

"Anyone contemplating trying to get a book written or published should stop right where you are and go out and buy Claudia Suzanne's *This Business of Books*. Intended for the novice, it contains excellent information about how the process works from beginning to end. It's a very realistic introduction to the book industry and covers writing and selling the manuscript to traditional publishers, or going the vanity press or do-it-yourself route.

"Suzanne provides rest stops and cautions along the way. If you don't know an ISBN from a LCCN, you need this publication. The book not only explains what these and other cryptic acronyms are, but tells you where and how to get them. The glossary and the text provide a wealth of information about publishing "lingo" that is well worth the price.

Prof. Daniel I. Morris, Greene County Messenger

"Aspiring Writers Should Read This Book"

"Many people dream of becoming successful authors. Many try to submit material to publishers or book agents, but their proposals or manuscripts are repeatedly rejected. Discouraged, they give up. I wish I'd had a copy of this book when we first decided to go into the business, even as a "hobby" or sideline."

Jon Baughman, B.T. Bulletin

"A "Must' For A Writer's Reference Library"

"'A complete overview of the industry from concept through sales.' A great understatement, to be sure. I intend to use it in my next class. The book's layout reflects an awareness of a writer's need for quick understanding of a multitude of subjects."

Shirl Thomas, writing instructor

"Writer Friendly Vs. Publisher Friendly"

"You cover everything a writer needs to know in order to make choices."

Louise Nelson, book publicist

"Any Would-Be Author Needs This Title"

"It imparts a variety of approaches to getting involved in the publishing industry, from work-for-hire situations to producing a book."

Diane Donovan, "Bookwatch"

"Invaluable Work"

"Claudia Suzanne provides a thorough overview of the industry."

Irwin Zucker, founder and former president,
Book Publicists of Southern California

"I Love It!"

"I've told everybody about this book."

Connie Clausen, literary agent (dec.)

This Business of Books

A Complete Overview of the Industry
From Concept Through Sales

4th Edition

Revised & Updated for the 21st Century

Claudia Suzanne

Printed in the United States of America

Publisher's Cataloging-in-Publication
 (Provided by Quality Books, Inc.)

Suzanne, Claudia.
  This business of books : a complete overview of the
industry from concept through sales / Claudia Suzanne.
 -- 4th ed., rev.& updated for the 21st century.
  p. cm.
  Includes index.
  LCCN 2003105862
  ISBN 0-9638829-4-5

  1. Book industries and trade--United States.
 2. Authorship. I. Title.

 Z471.S89 2003   381.45002'0973
                        QBI03-200792

WC Publishing
Tustin, California

Acknowledgements

No one writes and publishes any book all alone. My most heartfelt thanks go out to DC Hadden, for being my business manager, my advisor, my rock and my crisis-state counselor; Bera Dordoni, for being a perfect sister and an equally wonderful editor; Laurie Thomas for her incredible support, confidence and attention to detail; Ellen Van Houten and George Jenkins, for their constant reminders to stop and eat, stop and sleep, stop and breathe; Sonja Struthers, for helping me keep my eye on the ball and my spirits up; my parents, Pat and Mike Harris, and Carol J. Amato for their unflagging support; and most importantly, Tom and Lona, for making this whole thing worthwhile.

I am deeply grateful to Claire Reeves, Tim McCarthy, Michele Takai, Ph.D., and Ronald Zishka, Ph.D. for the use of their material contributions.

Finally, a special note of appreciation to Dan Poynter, Jerrold Jenkins, Jeff Herman, Elizabeth Pomada, Ellen Reid, Rabbi Bernie King, Amy Brandais, Salina Herrington, Julie Cavallo and Kristin Loberg for their gracious endorsement of this enterprise.

As for Squeak, Flake, Kit, Ziggy, AJ and Pablo: ha, ha, the book got finished anyway, despite your never-ending efforts to scratch my monitor, eat my optical mouse, scatter my notes around the office and leave your hairballs on my clean drafts!

To my students, for all their teaching
To my friends, for all their support
To my family, for all their love

Contents

Contents

1
A Touch Of Reality

Few industries have changed as much as book publishing has over the past few decades. We have new printing, new graphics and new production technologies. Publishing houses have merged, broken up and been bought up by both American and foreign conglomerates. Nevertheless, the fundamental realities of the business remain the same. Buying and selling books is still the same utterly subjective, personal-to-the-point-of-intimate trade it has always been, a world in which ordinary people wield authority totally out of proportion to any reason, based purely on their own tastes and their ability, at least occasionally, to pick a winning title. Agents decide if a project is worth pursuing using the hardly scientific criteria of, "Do I want to?" and "Do I think anyone else will, too?" And despite his most informed, experienced guesses, any agent worth his salt will tell you he rejects all but two or three percent of everything he receives, can only put a full-court press behind maybe two-thirds of what he does accept and will end up selling less than half of those, most for modest advances.

Acquisition editors employ a similar yardstick—is the book worth it? Is it professionally prepared? Will the author be capable and willing to help market it?—then add some calculations and projections about what has sold in the past and what the editorial chief would like to sell in the future. Look in any acquisition editor's reading pile, though, and you will see he's had to reject some wonderful manuscripts he really loved simply because trends and budget constraints make publishing two shorter titles more profitable than one large volume. The marketing department often holds final sway over the entire process, basing its decisions on spreadsheets, surveys and statistics that may or may not accurately predict what the reading public will be interested in six months to two years from now—and hoping it's right at least thirty to forty percent of the time.

In short, the book business is neither mysterious nor objective. It is a game in which new players come up to bat every day, the competition is fierce and there are lots and lots of rules you need to learn well so you can judiciously ignore them, as appropriate. There is no science to it, no empirical evidence of what always works and what never does; no guarantee that a well-written, compelling book will land a publisher and catch the public's eye, or that a poorly written title won't. The only continuity exists in the day-to-day tasks of each individual's specific job. If, indeed, life offers no absolutes, the book business is a perfect microcosm of that reality.

This is an industry in which powerful but nevertheless poorly written books have won national acclaim and international awards. Sentimental volumes so dripping with sweetness as to choke a honey bee have nonetheless captured the hearts and minds of millions upon millions of American readers, crossing all age, race, religion and gender lines. Complex, intricate texts on esoteric topics that would seemingly appeal only to the educated elite have shot to the top of the bestseller list and stayed there for months. Yet, anyone involved in even the lowest phase of the business knows of at least half-a-dozen finely crafted, extraordinary manuscripts that will never get traditionally published, because the business of writing and the business of publishing remain miles apart.

And it has always been thus.

Unlike any other arena, being a success in the book business does not necessarily translate to making great gobs of money. Authors of run-away bestsellers often cannot afford to quit their day jobs because all their advance money went to promotion and advertising costs. Genre writers may churn out one popular book after another, yet receive just enough compensation to live until the next deadline falls due. Of course, those with the right perspective and concentrated focus can indeed generate fortunes. Dan Poynter, the leading self-publishing expert, travels the country collecting speaker's fees and selling his regularly updated books by the case. Another self-publisher, who shall remain nameless, claims to earn millions of dollars every year by holding low-cost seminars on how to emulate the plain-design "how to" books he writes and sells through full-page advertisements and direct mailings. In other words, as in any industry, true entrepreneurs can develop successful, independent writing/publishing concerns that may not necessarily capture the general public's attention, but can certainly snag a large share of its disposable cash, especially if they don't rely on the profit-siphoning arena of retail bookstores.

We know about such cases because they are newsworthy; that is, they are sufficiently out of the ordinary to demand media attention. Most authors do not receive $1,000,000 for their first book; most lawyers do not land $4.2 million deals for penning a recap of a single trial. Yet when this week's bestseller drops off the Top-15 list; when the title that was going to revolutionize the self-help world has been edged off the market by a newer theory; when the latest marketing craze caves under to technological reality and that highly touted ebook winds up just another bunch of data bytes lost in cyber space, most of those authors will go back to their regular nine-to-five jobs while they try to snatch a few hours a day in which to write their next book.

This, too, has always been a book-industry reality.

Untraditional Tradition

For hundreds of years, publishers were individuals and companies whose main concern was making good literature and educational information available to the reading public.

As a business venture, publishing has historically been just this side of a bust. A firm could only expect to break even on perhaps half its books, and make an actual profit on possibly a third. It made sense to pick and choose those titles that seemed to have the greatest appeal to the widest audience.

Don't be fooled by sweet-talking scam artists—it still does.

Today's publishing world is divided into a number of layers that regularly encroach upon each other: traditional publishers, epublishers, vanity publishers, self-publishers and a murky group of entrepreneurs who claim to be part of one group (publishers) but are actually part of another (self-publishing service providers). Conventional wisdom tells us traditional publishers still produce between 50,000 and 70,000 books every year with self-publishers making up the balance of the approximately 120,000 titles released annually. One knowledgeable source, however, contends that small and independent publishers now account for some 78% of all published books. So which is the truth? Well....

If you are trying to get published by one of the major publishing houses, it feels better to think they still control at least half, if not most of the industry. If, on the other hand, you merely want to get published by a good firm, it makes sense to accept as reality that the major houses are constantly inundated with submissions, that cream cannot always rise to the top if it is overwhelmed by sheer volume and that a smaller publisher will be just as eager and committed as you are to making your book a popular and financial success.

It's all a matter of perspective.

New Options, Perpetual Order

Today, new publishing formats make dealing with a stack of technical or business manuals virtually hassle-free. The number of major publishers may have decreased, but most of their imprints are still intact, if relocated. Self-published titles are certainly more readily accepted in the marketplace. And while Barnes & Noble, Borders Books, Books-a-Million and Amazon.com may have driven thousands of independent booksellers out of business, more titles are now available to the general public at affordable prices than ever before in history.

Yet, though the old traditions of the publishing game have rearranged, expanded and adapted to new technologies, economic conditions and population demands, some aspects have remained indelibly the same, despite all the new names and merging phases. Contrary to dire predictions and hi-tech hoopla, books as we know them are not about to go out of style any time soon. We may have updated publishing formats, redirected distribution networks and creative new revenue streams, but hardcover and paper-bound books are still the most satisfying way to exercise the imagination and personalize any fantasy or drama. Paper-and-ink volumes that open with a fresh-book smell and can be fingered, hugged and tossed into a briefcase or purse without concern for battery discharge provide a tactile comfort and pleasure that pixels on a screen can never match. Books are not just knowledge or entertainment; they are personal items, intimate companions, precious possessions. The human animal has always had and will always have an insatiable desire to read, learn, grow, imagine and collect books.

2

Welcome To The 21st Century

Time was, only those who had a "calling" sat down to tackle the arduous task of writing a book. Their reasons for setting pen to paper were varied and heartfelt:

To communicate.

To chronicle their times.

To preserve their heritage.

To share a story or advance an idea or prove a point.

To touch other human beings.

To have an impact on society.

To leave their mark in the world.

To make some money.

The pursuit took time, skill and dedication. Each page had to be handwritten, scratched out, written over and re-written. Those with "natural" talent worked with their agents and editors to fine-tune every word, every idea, every plot twist and turn. Promising writers studied and read and honed their craft for decades before finally getting their first volume published, and accepted that process as the due course of the business. The pure labor involved in generating three hundred and fifty pages of clean manuscript literally took years of writing and copying. It was a solitary, lonely, physically, emotionally and spiritually taxing occupation.

But not anymore!

Today, Microsoft® and Intel® have effectively removed the drudgery from writing. Craft is prepackaged and compartmentalized; you can purchase by-the-number literary kits that provide story lines, plots and characters on floppy disk, CD-ROM and via online download. An energetic writer can whip out a three hundred and fifty-page manuscript in a couple of months, if not weeks, and clean it up with the help of Spell Check, Grammar Check, AutoCorrect and AutoFormat. Even the most remote areas of the world sport at least one or two writers' groups, and for those who cannot find a bunch of compatriots within driving distance, the Internet has more chat rooms, writers' sites, online courses, bulletin boards, message centers and news groups than any human could ever exhaust.

Yes, thanks to personal computing and the World Wide Web, all it takes is a little cash and you, too, can see your book in print, or at least in pixels. Not up to bucking the established system? Self-publish. Not enough cash or credit? ePublishing costs less than the price of a good book-release party. Still too much money? Post your work for free on a writers' group or bulletin board or your own web site. Promotion? Heck, anyone with enough chutzpah and perseverance can enjoy his fifteen minutes of fame on one of the hundreds of network, cable, regional or local TV or radio shows. Can't talk in front of a live audience? Let one of the thousands of online bookstores host a special-event "meet-the-author" chat for you.

Does all this mean that millions of people will read your words, get your message, and give you lots of money?

Oh my, no.

The brutal truth is, the number of ways for the untried, unproven aspiring author to get ripped off has increased tenfold. New scams arise daily for novice writers to waste their time, energy, money and hope. A beautiful website, an eBook or a POD (Print on Demand) novel or nonfiction book will still not reach significantly more people than if you had simply photocopied your work and handed it out to your family and friends. No matter how much money you spend, how quickly your home page loads or how professional your Adobe PDF file looks, your book will not rise above the fray;

you will not have communicated, touched, chronicled or shared.

To understand why, simply imagine this scenario. You have read every medical thriller you could get your hands on since childhood. You've watched every medically oriented movie and TV drama since "Dr. Kildare." You know the buzz words, you've had the diagnostic procedures, you recognize disease symptoms. Now as you walk into a surgical theater in hospital scrubs, you're faced with tubes and wires connected from an unconscious patient to various monitors, plastic bags and breathing machines—just like on every TV show you've ever seen. You stare down at the draped body. A nurse hands you a scalpel and says, "Make your first incision, Doctor."

Where will you put the point of the blade? How much pressure will you exert to cut through the skin and layers of muscle and fat? What will you do when the blood starts to spurt?

How will any of this help the patient?

Unless you are medically trained, you would probably never consider attempting such an irrational, presumptuous act, even with all your reading and movie watching and terminological knowledge. Yet most people approach writing a book as if they can simply draft a bestseller with nothing than a love of reading, a desire to be an author or a degree in English.

Bluntly put, there is a world of difference between the catharsis of keeping a stream-of-consciousness journal and the labor and skill involved in crafting a viable book that appeals to the reading public. That difference can only be bridged by hard work, talent and the type of mentorship inherent to every fine craft and trade. And yet, even outstanding books are not guaranteed a place on the bestseller lists in today's marketplace.

Wheat and Chaff

The next time you go to a party, meeting, political or religious event or even community picnic, bring up the subject of writing a book. Chances are, you will find at least one person who dreams about writing a love story, a tale of childhood, an opinion piece on some controversial topic or a title about some field of expertise. According to a 2002 survey, almost everyone—81% of the American public, in fact— regardless of age, financial status, race, background, religion or life circumstance, has something they want to share with the rest of the world. *Eighty-one percent of the American public!* That includes housewives, attorneys, journalists, physicians, CIA agents, psychiatrists, teachers, psychologists, social workers, CEOs, clerics, truck drivers, celebrities, entrepreneurs, college students, accountants, postal clerks and even sanitation workers, aka garbage collectors.

Most of that 81% will never write a book. Fewer will get published, and only a handful will see their titles become successful. The truth is, the difference between the many and the handful is not merely talent; many finely crafted, extraordinary manuscripts will never make it to the bookstores. Nor is it hard work and money, although you can certainly expend a good deal of both in the pursuit. No, what levels the playing field for writers in the book industry today is **knowledge**:

- Understanding the **ebb-and-flow** of the trade market;

- Recognizing when to **persevere** and when to be **flexible**;

- Appreciating the difference between fiction and nonfiction skills;

- And, most importantly, knowing better than to read only **nonfiction** but attempt to write **novels**.

Successfully published authors don't present themselves as authorities outside their range of expertise, or try to pen self-help books while they are still in the midst of searching for answers to their own crises. They pattern their books on what they've read, not the movies or television shows they've watched. They realize that creating a viable manuscript is less a matter of pounding out 350 pages of text than crafting a marketable product. Few do it alone; if truth be known, few ever did. Over fifty percent of all successful books today are worked on at some stage by a freelance ghostwriter, book doctor or consultant *before* they are sent out for submission or formatted for self-publication. As Frederick Praeger, president of Praeger Publishers so succinctly put it, "If it isn't good enough when we first see it, it doesn't get published."

Those freelance ghostwriters, book doctors, consultants and editors are part of a burgeoning "Editorial Services" industry that barely existed a few decades ago, when all editing and development was reserved for the book's publisher. Today, this unregulated, non-standardized industry covers a plethora of functional titles that have sprung up to explain exactly what part of the development/editing process will be addressed: rewrite, line editing, copy editing or proofreading. Titles get bandied about at each provider's discretion, often leaving writers confused. One person's definition of an editor, for example, is another person's concept of a book doctor; a third person's idea of proofreading is the same as someone else's understanding of copy editing. For the sake of brevity, this book will adhere to the definitions below.

Author

The **author** is that person whose ideas, stories, theories and so forth are the basis of the book, whether or not they[*] actually write the manuscript. An author is fully invested emotionally and financially in the outcome of the book. In the traditional literary field, the author developed, researched,

---

[*] To avoid the awkwardness of he or she or s/he, this book uses "they" and "their" as (historically correct) gender and number neutral.

wrote and rewrote his own manuscript, and could expect his publisher to edit and proofread it for him. In the modern book business, however, the author can and often does outsource everything from development to publishing, even when self-publishing, and may finance but not control all stages of distribution and promotion. The author's name always appears first on the cover, title page and copyright.

Ghostwriter

The modern **ghostwriter** begins with a book from its development stage, but is neither emotionally nor financially invested in the final product. The ghost takes either a flat fee or fee-plus-percentage. Some ghosts also take byline credit on their clients' books, but legally the ghostwriter's name is explicitly disallowed from appearing anywhere on the cover or copyright. Usually the ghost is merely noted or thanked in the book's Acknowledgements.

A ghost is one type of Editorial Services person to whom an aspiring author can outsource the actual labor of putting a book together, and may therefore also be involved with developing, writing, rewriting, doctoring and copy editing. The modern ghost's scope of responsibility stops there, however; ghosts adhere strictly to the aspiring author's material and voice throughout the book.

Traditional Ghost

Traditional ghosts either seek out knowledgeable and financially viable parties to collaborate on a specific kind of book, or are sought out by celebrities, CEOs, socially prominent individuals or government officials. In exchange for a fee and percentage of the advance/royalties, they create autobiographies, corporate white papers and "expert" books for their authors. In this classic form of ghosting, the ghost does all the research as well as the writing, rewriting, editing and submission or self-publication work, turning out a volume that may or may not read in the aspiring author's voice.

Because traditional ghosts are so deeply involved in the book from its inception and may even be the driving force behind the entire project, their emotional investment in the eventual success of the book may be as great as their authors'. High-profile clients have a significantly greater-than-normal chance of having their books accepted by major publishers and bought by large segments of the public.

Traditional Ghostwriting can be quite lucrative and satisfying. In fact, traditional ghosts are what most people think of when they hear the term "ghostwriter." As such, it comes with the obvious limitation inherent in that definition: high-profile, deep-pocketed clients comprise only a small percentage of the millions of aspiring authors, winnowing your potential client pool down from millions to thousands, if not merely hundreds. What's more, your competition is fiercer, since you're going up against the elite group of established, well-connected professional ghosts who already write for the rich and famous. Nevertheless, if you have the skills, the knowledge and, most importantly, the connections or ability to make those connections, writing for the rich and famous is a nice way to secure your industry reputation and feed your KEOGH or IRA.

Book Doctor/Line Editor

No one is quite sure where the term originated, but **Book Doctor** is the current vernacular for the historical title "**line editor**," or simply "**editor**." Doctoring is a mid-range task that is deeper than simple copy editing but less intricate or involved than ghostwriting or collaborating. Paid for by flat fee or per-hour rate, it requires no emotional investment in the book. Book doctors/line editors come to the project after the content has been fully developed, structured and written, and are concerned with everything from internal structure, to converting passive voice into active prose, on down to grammar and copy editing. A book doctor may get "edited by" credit on the cover or title page of the book, but is usually only recognized in the Acknowledgements, if at all.

Copy Editor

When someone says a book needs to be edited, most people think about applying the kind of "rules" English teachers advocate: correcting grammar, punctuation, word choice, and so forth. This is the work of the **Copy Editor**. A copy editor generally charges by the hour or page, and will proofread at the same time if he is a cold reader—that is, someone who has not previously seen the manuscript at all. Copy editors seldom get byline credit, although they may be recognized in the Acknowledgements.

Proofreader

Proofreading is an often misunderstood but essential job, exclusively concerned with finding any lingering typographical errors in the final polished draft of the manuscript. Ergo, the **Proofreader** must be a cold reader to find minute errors; a familiar reader's brain will automatically "see" what it knows is supposed to be there.

Professional Book Writer™

Professional Book Writers, or PBWs, can perform all the above functions, from author/writer to copy editor and proofreader.

Professional Book Writer™ is a trademark-pending designation that indicates the individual has completed a specific course of study and mentored training.

> For information on becoming a Professional Book Writer, call 1-800-641-3936 or go to www.pbws.org.

The Phases

One other aspect of the book business has remained the same throughout all the technological updates and expanding service markets. The life of any book still goes through eight distinct phases:

1. Concept
2. Writing
3. Submissions
4. Publishing
5. Distribution
6. Marketing
7. Author Promotion
8. Sales (Fulfillment)

The remainder of this book will examine each of these phases in turn.

3

Concept

A book's concept is more than just the **topic** or fictional **theme** of the work; it also includes the **audience** for which it is geared, the **type** of book it is and the **category** into which it falls.

Topic

What you communicate is as important as how you communicate. Writing reflects your flavor or soul as an author, so pick topics that excite your imagination, wonder or curiosity, and avoid accepting assignments or projects in which you have little or no interest. This may sound like a banal warning, but many writers have "sold their souls for a mess of pottage," and ended up writing books that were agonizing to work on for a sum of money that was spent before the project was ever completed.

While no topic can be justly labeled invalid and the smallest piece of work on the most obscure subject can be of gut-wrenching importance to the person producing it, four hundred and fifty pages on something only a tiny percentage of the population would care to read about is passion, not reason, talking. On the other hand, always writing for the public's pleasure and never for yourself produces a cold, frustrated existence. The ideal scenario, of course, occurs when a writer's area of interest and expertise coincides with the appetite of a large segment of the public.

"Write What You Know"

Probably the most oft-repeated admonition in the writing field, "write what you know" does not mean you should only write about those things and feelings already in your life. A better paraphrase would be, "know what you write." Specifically, you need familiarity with the feel, taste, sound, smell and sight of the subject, be it a murder mystery or a nonfiction history of King George III's reign. Writing is not a fast craft; when you are dealing with an unfamiliar theme, you may have to conduct extensive research to compensate for the information ordinarily accumulated over years of participation or study. Take the time to investigate not only the core of the subject, but also those tangent areas that affect the feel or direction of the business. In recent years, dozens of books have been set in Orange County, California, for example, because the authors live there and know the feel of the place. Take a lesson from any good biography, which invariably begins not with the subject's childhood years, but with the background of the individual's parents as well. By exploring the source, or heritage of a subject or person, you gain the insight you will need to interpret and communicate.

More Than An Idea

Along those lines, realize that simply having the idea does not constitute a fully developed topic or theme. For both writing and sales purposes, you need a larger image of what the book will be about than, for example, "a love story" or "exploring space." The more you understand the story you want to tell or the theories you want to discuss, the better the chance you will accomplish your goal. A novel about "romance in South America," for instance, is not as well defined as "a young couple finding love while caring for the orphaned children in POVerty-stricken Honduras." Likewise, "exploring space" hardly nails down the book's contents, whereas "exploring our galaxy through the eyes of a child" does.

> ## Did You know?
> Ridley Pearson got the idea for writing Diary of Ellen Rimbauer: My Life at Rose Red (Hyperion, 2002) after reading the script for his friend Stephen King's ABC mini-series, Red Rose. "'Ridley read the script, and noticed that a diary was mentioned repeatedly, so he went to Steve and said, 'why don't I just write the diary?' By all accounts, King thought it was a great idea."
> Dena Croog, PW Daily for Booksellers (June 27, 2002)

Audience

Who will read your book must be taken into consideration before you start writing. Writing for academics or professionals requires a different focus and more specialized or sophisticated language than writing for the trade public; writing for children is obviously different from writing for adults. When you write for children, you must also know what age group or school level you are targeting. Most writers know their audience without giving it much thought, but sometimes a novelist, for example, will create something he thinks is for adults but will actually appeal more to a young-adult audience. Professionals who sit down to write a book based on their years of clinical study or experience may write for their colleagues yet want to sell to the public. Writing is about decisions: make this one before you start the creative process.

Type and Category

A book can be one of seven types: Reference, Text, Trade Nonfiction, Religious, Literary Fiction, Poetry or Trade Fiction. Within those types, however, are an almost endless number of categories.

Historically, **reference books** were encyclopedias, dictionaries, almanacs and similar all-in-one volumes of facts, dates and figures. Today, we have computer and software manuals, where-to-find-everything-on-the-net guides, free-grants-for-all-occasions listings, and hundreds of other inventive daily and business research tools that get updated on a regular basis. Some author/writers even produce successful reference books that explain *other* reference books. Carol J. Amato's *World's Easiest Guide to Using the APA*, for instance, clarifies the APA Style Manual, which dictates how certain academic term papers, theses and dissertations must be formatted. Reference categories and searchable ebooks are a match made in technological heaven.

Textbooks are constantly updated and replaced, especially in the upper levels of traditional education. With education becoming a lifelong pursuit rather than a twelve-or sixteen-year duty, the adult-education and college-extension subcategory has opened vast new frontiers for textbook writers. While parent committees, school boards and state requirements dictate all elementary through high school (el-hi) textbook purchases, individual departments and teachers make their own post-secondary textbook decisions.

Trade Nonfiction is that large, sweeping range of books geared for the reading public, whether targeted at a broad spectrum of readers or a small niche of the general market. Nonfiction categories include—but are not limited to—agriculture, arts, biography/autobiography, business, education, general works, history, home economics, language, law, medicine, music, philosophy/psychology, science, sociology/economics, sports/recreation, technology and travel. Trade nonfiction has an inherently short shelf life; unless it addresses a universal topic in a timeless manner, it will soon be replaced when a new author comes up with a fresh approach to the same subject.

Religious books include the Christian Bible, Jewish Tanakh, Islamic Qur'an, Hindu Rig Veda, Buddhist Dhammapada, et cetera, as well as their various codicils, interpretations and commentaries and the inspirational true-life stories, attacks/debates and religious or spiritual novels they inspire.

Literary Novels and **Poetry** hold a special place in today's book world. While their authors seldom see the kind of advance money or immediate sales figures that trade-book authors like J.K. Rowling or John Grisham enjoy, they do compete better for prestigious honors and can conceivably look forward to longer shelf lives. Most writing prizes and grants are awarded to poetry and literary novels rather than popular fiction, a fact that has caused a good deal of controversy on occasion. Furthermore, while techno-action/adventure is a strong-selling trade subcategory, Jane Austin's *Pride and Prejudice* probably has a better chance of still being read in 2103 than Tom Clancy's *Hunt for Red October*.

The last category, **Trade Fiction**, comprises children's titles from picture books through Harry Potter, as well as both genre and mainstream adult fiction.

Genre refers to those stories that adhere to a specific theme, such as Romance, the largest-selling category of adult fiction; or contain specific circumstances, such as Sci-Fi, or recognizable elements, such as Fantasy. A loosely used term, it can also refer to any kind of book where the specific nature of the material is the most prominent feature: action/adventure, horror/suspense, erotica, mystery, western, military, gothic, gay/lesbian, and so on.

The exact nature of genre is difficult to nail down. Mysteries, for example, one of the oldest genres, are traditionally told from the detective's point of view (POV), regardless of whether that character is actually a housewife, restaurant reviewer or licensed private eye. The crime appears quite early in the book and the detective encounters plenty of red herrings (misleading clues) and suspects, but the real culprit (or culprits) is often among the least suspected or even over-looked characters even though clues pointing to his guilt are sprinkled throughout the book.

In contrast, a mainstream novel that involves a mystery may contain red herrings and a boatload of suspects, but does not necessarily have to keep the bad guy unknown until the end of the book. In fact, novels that let the reader know "who done it" early in the book often derive their fun from the protagonist and antagonist trying to circumvent each other for two-hundred and fifty pages. But are they genre? Probably not.

Fantasy, another popular genre, uses specific kinds of characters, settings and events that would normally have to be explained in a mainstream novel. Griffins, for example, appear in many if not most popular contemporary fantasies, so the author can expect her readers to already have knowledge of their appearance and traits. If a griffin appeared in a mainstream novel, however, the author could not make that kind of assumption, and would have to describe the creature as half eagle, half lion.

Today, bookstores shelve their titles by the loosely grouped genres noted above, and combine all non-genre novels under something like "Literature and Contemporary Fiction." Anything that does not fit into one of the predetermined classifications is relegated to these shelves, which consequently amounts to a mixture of classic literature and current novels that appeal to the general reading public. Look around most bookstores, however, and you'll see they mirror the statistical reality that trade fiction only accounts for 12-14% of any given year's publishing.

> **Did You know?**
>
> Two basic elements comprise every romance novel: a central love story and an emotionally satisfying and optimistic ending.
>
> A Central Love Story—In a romance, the main plot concerns two people falling in love and struggling to make the relationship work. The conflict in the book centers on the love story. The climax in the book resolves the love story. A writer is welcome to as many subplots as she likes as long as the relationship conflict is the main story.
>
> An Emotionally Satisfying and Optimistic Ending—Romance novels end in a way that makes the reader feel good. Romance novels are based on the idea of an innate emotional justice—the notion that good people in the world are rewarded and evil people are punished. In a romance, the lovers who risk and struggle for each other and their relationship are rewarded with emotional justice and unconditional love.
>
> Once the central love story and optimistic-ending criteria are met, a romance novel can be set anywhere and involve any number of plot elements.
>
> (reprinted with permission of
> Romance Writers of America
> http://www.rwanational.org/romance.stm)

Concept Initiators

While it is a pretty thought that all books are the result of author inspiration and passion, it is also a myth. The concept of a book can come from:

- the **author**, whether or not he intends to actually write the book himself
- a **co-author** or **collaborator** who, also, may or may not intend to write the book
- an **employer**, defined as any entity or individual that hires a writer, usually on a work-for-hire basis, to develop and write a book

- a **publisher**, who assigns one or a series of concepts, sometimes on a work-for-hire basis, sometimes on a traditional or modified royalty basis, to one or more author/writers

- a **packager**, who might contract a stable of author/writers, again either on a work-for-hire or royalty basis, to write a series of books he then designs, produces, duplicates and delivers to a publishing house

- an **attorney**, **agent** or other **middleman** who puts authors and writers together, pitches ideas to writers or arranges package deals between publishers, authors and professional book writers.

When a non-writing author or co-author originates the concept, he must either learn to write, find a writing collaborator or hire a Professional Book Writer™ (PBW). PBWs, however, have the option to create their own book projects, contract their services or explore the alternatives of Assignments or Work Made for Hire.

Assignments

Assignments are book projects handed out either by publishers or packagers, also known as producers. Packagers handle all aspects of producing the book, from initializing the concept through binding the copies. They outsource the manuscript to one or more writers, the illustrations and graphics to artists/designers, the formatting/typesetting to a design house and the duplication and binding to a book manufacturer or POD printer. In the past, most packagers turned the book over to the publisher at this point; today, many also get involved with contracting promotional, publicity and advertising services.

Packaging is most economical for a series of titles that all use the same design and format and are targeted for the same market, such as elementary and secondary textbooks or a trade-science series. The publisher does not have to deal with individual manuscripts, nor expend the man-hours or production budget normally required to put its imprint on a professionally edited, designed and produced series of books. Writers can start or expand their credit list without having to come up with their own ideas or compete for a publisher's attention. Packagers are often able to produce multiple volumes faster than publishers without maintaining a large facility and staff, because they can outsource almost all of the required writing, editing, design and production services.

Publishers are another source of book-length assignments. Some handle one kind of title exclusively, such as children's books, textbooks, travel books, general-education books, technical manuals, computer games and so on. Others specialize in direct-market books, and need a steady supply of fresh titles, if not topics, so their catalogs will always look new and current.

Publishers and packagers who offer assignments rely on a fluctuating stable of writers to whom they provide guidelines regarding content, length, chapter size, language, audience and completion deadline. After reviewing the parameters, the writer submits a chapter-by-chapter outline of the book and, sometimes, a sample first chapter. If the material is acceptable, the writer is paid part of an advance, which usually ranges from five hundred to five thousand dollars. The balance of the advance is either paid upon acceptance of the complete manuscript or at the time of publication. Once a writer has established a good relationship with a publisher or packager, query and proposal requirements may relax, and fees may rise.

To obtain an assignment, submit samples that illustrate your writing skill and your ability to conform to grade-level perception and language. Assigned books usually bear the name of the writer, are copyrighted by the publisher in the name of the writer, and either pay the low end of the royalty scale or are produced as work-for-hire.

A Unique Situation

Work-for-hire is a special circumstance in which an employer controls and reaps the benefits of his employees' creations, known in legal terms as intellectual property, in return for a set amount of money and the benefits of being an employee. Specifically, it refers to any work prepared by an employee within the scope of his employment, be it writing, visual or graphic art, film production, sound, software, chemical compound, genetic synthesis or any other product, device or theory.

Many creative people consider work-for-hire degrading and unfair, especially those who develop new products that increase company sales or send their corporation's stock soaring while they receive nothing more than an "attaboy" for their efforts. In the case of freelance writing, work-for-hire means a loss of copyright although not necessarily byline; payment on the employer's terms, not the writer's; and no control over the eventual outcome of the product, sometimes even as far as reviewing edits or allowing revisions. A work-for-hire writer cannot sell, resell or reproduce the material in any form—certainly not in situations for profit.

The vast majority of work-for-hire writers used to be actual corporate employees who enjoyed company benefits and whose job descriptions included writing. Hence, whatever they created for a corporate project was considered "part of the job" and, therefore, deemed reasonable for the corporation to retain. Then the market changed, and freelance writers started hiring themselves out to corporations or accepting repeated assignments from publishers and packagers in return for a guaranteed fee. Subsequently, the Supreme Court put limits on work-for-hire in an effort to impose some equity on those situations. Conservatively applying the letter of the law, the court ruled that the work-for-hire stipulation can only apply in actual employer/employee situations as defined and used in general common law. If you specifically agree in writing to relinquish copyright claim in exchange for other considerations, then the copyright holder, be it corporation, publisher or packager, may be liable to provide you with actual employee benefits. In California, for example, work-for-hire employees are entitled to state-sponsored unemployment insurance, workers' compensation benefits and disability insurance for the duration of the contract, even if the employer is located in another state.

In brief, whether a given circumstance is a work-for-hire or contracted situation depends on:

- Who has the right to control the writer's skill, work location, role in hiring and paying assistants and tax treatment

- Whether the writer is in business for himself or receives employee benefits

- Whether the employer has the right to assign additional projects to the writer or must negotiate them on an individual basis

While no specific law states that an employer must accept your made-for-hire work, standard practice is to pay the writer whether or not the material gets published. Work-for-hire assignments are a no-risk opportunity to hone your book-writing skills and acquire some titles for your credit list.

4
Writing

While this book is not meant to be a substitute for a creative-writing class or composition seminar, let's face it: "Writing" is the one phase around which all other book-business activity revolves. Consequently, this section is less a primer than a succession of helpful tips, tricks, definitions and explanations. First, though, let's pause for a moment of reflection.

Eighteenth-century British writer and lexicographer Samuel Johnson once claimed that, "No man but a blockhead ever wrote except for money." That sentiment still applies today; most writers want to sell their work. Yet, even with all the labor-reducing advances of the last half-century, most book writers do not open their veins and bleed on the paper just for the cash. They write because writing is their life—writing is who they are, what they need to do, how they express themselves. Serious wordsmiths spend their lives perfecting their craft, developing their art and learning about their business. They are aware of their own talent, potential and limitations, and are able to recognize the difference between filling a page with words and crafting a manuscript that can touch another person's soul. Ergo, the phrase "serious writer" refers not to the type of story or nonfiction you produce, but to the attitude you have toward your work and career. And political incorrectness notwithstanding, you can expect your fellow writers, the agents you solicit, the publishers to whom you pitch and the critics who review your book to examine your literary conduct.

Most fields of endeavor have, in their ideal state, a code of ethics to guide participants along the path of honesty, fairness and contribution. Of course, one need only watch the news or read the papers to see how well those ethical codes work in modern politics, business or even, to many people's chagrin, journalism. Nevertheless, you can charge a doctor with malpractice or take a plumber to court over a job poorly done because those occupations are regulated by professional or trade codes of ethics along with dozens of federal and state regulations. A person cannot call himself an attorney if he hasn't passed the bar exam.

In contrast, the only laws governing the written word have to do with intellectual property aspects such as copyright infringement and plagiarism and socio-political aspects such as slander or libel. Publishers may have to abide by fair-practice regulations, but not writers. Printers may have to conform to truth-in-advertising laws, but not writers. Journalists can *make up stories* and know the worst they'll have to face is losing their job. Even though the written word is the most enduring form of communication, affecting lives and events today, tomorrow and, potentially, for hundreds of years to come, no law mandates that you write the truth.

And many people don't—yet another historical reality.

Nevertheless, most serious writers do adhere to an unwritten set of standards that cautions us to hold to honesty, if not truth, and write so as to command respect and reflect honor upon the profession. Words like "respect" and honor" may sound arcane and impractical in light of the scandals and terrors of the modern era, but you'll find they matter a great deal to your fellow wordsmiths, many of whom you will meet (and need) as you grow and develop. Since "crisis plus observation equals truth," ethical behavior is most critical when temptations are greatest. Your behavior under stress demonstrates your reliability and trustworthiness, especially since you cannot hope to maintain a reading audience based on sloppy work, a career based on deceit or a sense of self-respect based on self-deception.

Know Your Craft

Craft requires practice, persistence and patience, for learning to write means writing, rewriting, re-rewriting and still more writing. Rather than imply that beginning writers cannot or should not try to sell, "knowing your craft" means that sales should never mark the end of learning.

Write To Communicate

Regardless of perspective, subject or style, text should be written in clear, understandable language using readable sentence structure. Let the message be more important than the words used to convey it.

Write With Honesty

All individuals see the truth in terms of their own lives; being honest about that personal truth is the power behind fine writing. In more practical terms, honesty means not cheating the audience with characters who act without motivation, crimes that get solved from clues not previously exposed or conclusions arrived at through fallacy-ridden, contrived or illogical arguments.

Honesty can be scary, because it means you must allow yourself to be vulnerable. Those hidden, secret, protected parts of your psyche are what will resonate with your readers, not your restrained, impersonal or impartial information. In fact, the "academic" writing used in so many textbooks probably explains why so many kids go to such lengths to avoid reading them.

Be Original

Writing is not for the shy or faint-at-heart. Readers develop a "feel" for an author far more by the words on the page than by the short biography on the back of the dust jacket. Lifting another author's style is as much of a deceit as plagiarizing someone else's words, unless, of course, you are ghostwriting for that author. Then again, using that other style as a foundation can help you develop a new, personal expression through which your own essence can shine. This truth has been proven in recent years on thousands of Internet fan-fiction (fanfic) sites, where, as usual, the cream manages to find its way to the top.

Write With Courage

No statement exists—including this one—that cannot be challenged by someone in some way for some reason. If you find yourself worrying about whom you are going to offend with your honesty, cast about for another occupation. By the same token, the written word can cause a great deal of harm, and has been credited historically with starting wars, bringing down great leaders and creating widespread panic. There's a very fine line between honesty and exploitation; you can straddle it, but recognize the consequences if you decide to cross it.

Give Credit Where Credit Is Due

When you quote, get the person's permission first. When you rely on researched material, list your sources. When you accept help on a manuscript, acknowledge the contribution. When you collaborate, refer to the authorship as "we," not "I."

Honor Commitments

This refers to both written and oral agreements, so avoid making commitments that cannot be honored due to time constraints, conflict of interest or ability. Do not claim to be a fiction editor if you do not read novels; do not promise to make a deadline if you know it is beyond your reach; do not ever promise a client that a book will sell unless you have proof of forthcoming divine intervention.

Respect Confidences

Though it is true that writers are notorious for storing everything they see and hear for later use, remember that part of your art is the ability to disguise. If you've been given permission to use a story but not the name of the person who contributed it, suppress any social, professional or physical attributes that might reveal the contributor's identity. When you collaborate on material that involves a new and/or secret focus or technique, refrain from discussing the work in progress, even with friends and family. When you listen to a friend's intimate tale of personal tragedy or embarrassment, don't make the often tragic mistake of automatically assuming the story can be "lifted" and retold in print.

> ## Did You Know?
> On December 13, 2002, Columbia University rescinded Michael Bellesile's Bancroft Prize for his book *Arming America* (Vintage) and requested the ex-Emory professor return the $4,000 award money. Columbia discovered that the author had suppressed research that did not support his thesis.
>
> PW Daily for Booksellers, December 16, 2002

Be Honest About Yourself

Don't magnify your credits or contributions beyond the facts; don't accept assignments under false pretenses; don't convey untrue or inaccurate impressions about your abilities or interests. This is a tricky area in today's marketplace, where an author can pay for 100 Print-on-Demand (POD) copies of a novel and call herself a published novelist, even if her reading audience only extends to family and friends. The truth will out eventually, and in the bottom-line book business, deceit clings and can destroy a writer's reputation.

Be Honest With Yourself

If a piece of writing is bad, discard it. If the work is not up to par by deadline, admit it. And if the project is simply too difficult for you, seek help.

Cultivate Literacy

Writers are expected to understand proper grammar, decent sentence structure and correct word usage, and to have a good command of the language. Such confinements do not, of course, dictate formality, style, tense, voice or educational level, but rather enjoin against incorrect or illogical usage, common though they may be. For example, although used interchangeably on television, "presently" does not mean "currently"; "I could care less" certainly does not convey the idea that you *couldn't* care less; and "He was really unique" is redundant, as a thing either is or is not unique.

In an attempt to demonstrate a sophisticated or educated vocabulary, aspiring authors sometimes resort to the thesaurus, their word-processor's synonym list or their own imaginations so as to sprinkle "impressive" terms throughout their manuscripts. The result is usually jarring, silly or just plain wrong.

"He set up a mendacious meeting."

"She sat at her directoire desk."

"If you ever obtrude on me again when I'm shaving, I'll tan your hide!"

Know your craft!

5

Nonfiction

Aspiring authors are often stymied when they first sit down to write their nonfiction book: "I've got this great idea, but I don't know how to get started." The simplest solution is to break the project down into a five-step process: 1) research, 2) structure, 3) write first draft, 4) rewrite and 5) format and edit.

Much of the "magic" of the book is created in the first two steps, research and structure, yet many first-time writers leapfrog from idea to first draft to editing, often spending a great deal of time and money on precise editing when the manuscript still needs restructuring and rewriting. And though thousands of books are written by authors who do not consciously adhere to this particular method or who use techniques promoted in other writing manuals and classes, this process has a unique advantage: it effectively eliminates writer's block.

Step 1: Research

Nonfiction research is almost a "given" for most first-time authors. They seldom have to go to lengths to research their books, as they've lived with their theories or ideas for years and are constantly conducting research as part of their daily efforts. The MFCC who wants to write a book on family dynamics, for example, has probably been developing her take on the subject over the course of her entire career. The history professor has been gathering information for his book about George Washington since he first developed a passion for the Revolutionary War.

Traditional ghosts and author/writers who accept assignments, however, will sometimes have to gather information on topics about which they have no frame of reference. Suppose, for example, you are offered an assignment by a children's publisher to create a seventy to 100-page book on the history of transportation, geared to the seventh or eighth-grade level. You've never written on this subject before, nor do you belong to an automobile, boating or train society or subscribe to *Car and Driver* or any other industry-oriented publication. Still, the idea of tracing modes of transportation from the earliest forms to the most recent stages of supersonic jets, bullet trains and space aeronautics fascinates you. You accept the assignment and develop a plan of research.

Your first step is to uncover the different kinds of transport used throughout history, starting with man's first method of moving from one place to the next—walking. You then explore how different societies relied on different inventions as the centuries progressed, including those that were used only for brief periods, but added to the general knowledge and forward progression of the subject.

Your next step is to discover, if possible, who originated those different devices, and what their lives were like before and after. What were they originally trying to accomplish? What were their motivations? Did their inventions fulfill their dreams? What about the people who used wind-powered carts and dug-out canoes—how did those inventions change lives? How did those lives change their societies, and, subsequently, history? What effect did the historical changes have on the next phase of the transportation chronicle?

By the time your research is finished, you will have a strong knowledge of the times and cultures that correspond to each step in the transportation chain, and will know about history from a feet-to-spacecraft perspective, with insight into the dispersion of humankind across the great continents and the effects of the industrial revolution had on transportation modes. You'll know about the X-Prize, war wagons, legal battles, horse thieving, wind sailing, and the invention of the wheel. In other words, you will know far, far too much to fully recount in a 100-page book for junior-high readers. In fact, only about 10% of what you have learned will end up in your final manuscript, a percentage considered wholly appropriate for this type of book. But you will be able to communicate a unique and fascinating perspective in what might otherwise have been a rather boring, same-old-same-old reference book.

With everything you learned doing research for this one assignment, you can easily reorganize, restructure and submit a proposal for a complementary volume, focusing on one or two especially intriguing periods, progressions, inventors, or inventions. This is called "turn-around"—using a single set of research material to write several articles, an article and a book or a series of books. Turn-around writing is one of the more profitable tricks-of-the-trade for professional writers, and explains why nonfiction book writers often also have many magazine articles to their credit. Even if you do not use your supplementary material for a turn-around volume, gathering it all was nonetheless essential. Insufficient researching leads to strained, thin writing, the kind that bores readers and causes manuscript rejection.

Interviewing

In the course of your research, you may need to conduct one or more interviews. Many ghosted memoirs or autobiographies, for example, are created entirely from taped interviews. Other nonfiction books can also benefit from interviews with people besides the author. Information gathered first-hand from established experts or persons deeply involved in a given field can provide a stronger understanding of the attitudes and emotions inherent to a subject, plus give you the added advantage of primary-source quotes. Even if you do not quote your experts, their perspective can add dimension, insight and vigor to the project.

Interviews can be pre-arranged or spur-of-the-moment, conducted in person, by phone, via fax or through e-mail. For a live interview, prepare yourself with specific questions, a tape recorder and a notepad.

Specific Questions

Jot down both general and specific questions for easy referral. The list must be flexible—you may not use all the questions, and others may occur to you during the course of the conversation. In some instances, the subject may correct misconceptions or provide additional information beyond your specific inquiries. If the subject contradicts previous data, you may need to do additional research and interviewing.

Tape Recorder

Recording ensures quote and general-impression accuracy. If you expend all your concentration taking detailed notes during an interview, you cannot focus on the subject's facial or hand expressions, body language, tone of voice, emphasis or flow of the conversation. Voice-activated recorders use less tape than those that run continuously and are, consequently, less cumbersome to transcribe. The activation-volume switch must be turned up high enough to catch the beginnings of sentences. Telephone interviews can be recorded by use of an inexpensive connective device, available at most audio stores. As of this writing, voice-recognition software still requires attenuation to a single speaker, so using a laptop to directly transcribe the interviewee's words is not yet feasible. In the few months it will take for this book to hit the market, of course, technology may have cleared that hurdle.

Notepad

Even though the tape is going, you will still want to record your observations of the interviewee's emotional responses, physical characteristics, gestures, emphasis, and so forth as well as any questions that occur to you while the subject is talking. Rather than interrupt, jot down your question(s) and come back to them before going on to the next item on your list.

Tips

Do not interrupt the interviewee, if possible. Start by asking him about the first topic on the list, then let him talk without stopping for questions. Unless he needs prompting, jot your questions or points of interest down to ask after he stops talking, then cover those questions fully before you go on to the next point on the list.

Interviewing can be a fits-and-starts proposition, especially if you are writing a memoir or autobiography. Schedule plenty of time for every session in a multiple-interview project so you can socialize for a while, have a cup of coffee, use the facilities and so forth. If you are dealing with a professional who wants to create an "expert" book, make sure the interviews take place in a quiet room away from interruptions. Do not try to squeeze the interviews in on a lunch hour at the interviewee's desk unless all land and cell phones are turned off, the door is locked and you both have enough lunch hours to cover fully everything you need to know.

Quotes

Fear of quoting someone without their knowledge can be as much of a barrier to composition as disregarding someone's rights can be a legal imposition. Recent court rulings, for example, have denied journalists the right to "piece" together a quote from separate interviews without the interviewee's consent, especially if the new configuration shows the person in a bad light. All this legal hassle can be avoided with a little common sense, and a basic commitment to fair play. As a rule of thumb, the following sources **can** be quoted:

Remarks or statements you have personally heard, provided you report them accurately and they were not specifically noted to be "off the record." This would cover remarks spoken during a personal, televised, or radio-broadcast interview.

Remarks previously published. Statements made in magazine interviews, for example, can be repeated word for word provided the source of the quote is noted as such: "I wouldn't want it any other way," the actress said in a 1989 *Newsweek* interview.

Previously published letters, articles or books, as long as you obtain permission in advance from the author and/or publisher.

Letters, notes, or memos you personally received. Similar material sent to a third person is the property of that individual; consequently, you must obtain that person's permission for reprint rights, not the original author of the piece.

The following **cannot** be quoted without risk of legal entanglement:

Individuals unaware their remarks are being noted for publication, and/or who have not given you permission to record their statements.

Remarks made in confidence and overheard or repeated by a third party.

Remarks taken sufficiently out of context so as to change the original intent or meaning, such as piecing together contradictory remarks from two separate interviews to give the impression they were made at the same time.

Any material taken from the internet without permission and/or citation. The operative term in that warning is "citation." By citing the source and specific URL, you demonstrate that the material was previously published and, as such, quotable. However, since the courts have not yet resolved all the various Internet rights issues, use a little common sense when quoting from the web, and apply the same guidelines as if quoting from a printed source: give credit where due, and when in doubt, get written permission.

Step 2: Structure

Structuring nonfiction means creating a logical sequence of information, or "slinky flow," so that one idea follows another from beginning to end, the way a slinky "walks" down one step after another until it hits the bottom of the stairs or a midway ledge. A slinky flow allows the reader to follow your theory from its starting point to its conclusion, or to understand how a stated theory applies in various circumstances. When a nonfiction book's slinky flow hits a ledge, the reader stops reading. Unless the work is so compelling that he picks it up again on his own, the entire purpose of the book—to communicate your ideas—is thwarted. Using the technique below will help you avoid structural ledges.

List All Ideas

Record everything you want to cover in the manuscript, either from your research findings and/or transcripts or your own brainstorming. If you are doing a memoir, list all the incidents you want to include. If you are advancing a theory, note all the points you want to cover. Do not try to write paragraphs or even full sentences; confine yourself to a few words on each idea. Jot the points down in whatever order they come, and don't get concerned if new ideas occur to you over a period of several days or even weeks; writing a first manuscript is not a speedy endeavor. Just keep making notations until you're sure you have a complete list of everything you want to discuss in your book.

This starting point is especially vital when creating a manuscript from interviews and notes. You absolutely must have a list of the book's contents from which to work, even if you are working with an author who assures you she knows exactly what she wants to say and can simply extemporize.

Order the Topics

Separate the ideas into groupings, the groupings into sections and the sections into an outline. If you are working off a previously written manuscript, do a quick outline of what already exists. If you are developing the manuscript, create a slightly more in-depth framework. You need not get overly intricate at this point. When creating a manuscript from taped interviews and notes, use this outline to guide your recording sessions.

Expound

Now is the time to insert **placeholders** for your research into the proper slots, or simply start expanding on the outline you've created. A placeholder is nothing more than a few lines or a blurb that indicates the depth of the material you will insert later. By broadening the outline before you start writing, you'll discover if you've forgotten anything as you go from topic to topic. Do not try to create the manuscript at this point; just expand on the ideas, one after the other, until you've got a complete digest of the material from beginning to end. The result can be anywhere from twenty to eighty pages.

Restructure

With the information gained by expanding the original outline, create a map of the entire book, using the following format for each chapter with sub-heads included as necessary.

    a.   Topic introduction

b. Ensuing discussion [stated briefly or outlined in detail]

c. Topic resolve

d. **Transition** to next topic

Transitions support structure. If you cannot transition from Idea A to Idea B, you are either missing material, have put the material in the wrong order or are ready for a chapter or section break.

Transitions relate the current discussion to the succeeding one, smoothly connecting one part of the work to the next, with the emphasis on smoothly. If the information flows for several chapters and then leaps to another topic altogether— if there is, in fact, no smooth way to connect or relate the former discussion to the latter—then section the book. You can also use sections when you want to emphasize the division of material. Just remember to put the sections in logical order.

Step 3: The First Draft

In your first pass on the material, don't worry about careful wording, nice editing or final formatting, and don't get overwhelmed by how little you accomplish in a single day or how much is left to be done. No one can sit down and write a book. You can only write one chapter at a time.

Make sure the chapters are complete within themselves, with or without subheads. The key issue at this stage is to remember you are writing a first draft. Translation: it *will* be rewritten. Be careful not to drive yourself crazy trying to create a perfect first chapter before moving on in the book. The only thing you want to do with the first chapter of the first draft is get the information down, even if the prose is disjointed and sloppy. First chapters are always rewritten after the entire manuscript is on paper.

If you develop writer's block during the first draft, most likely:

- Your structure needs to be reworked
- You have a "hole" in your pool of information
- You are trying to stuff material to which you are emotionally attached into a book in which it does not belong
- You either are not being honest or not allowing yourself to be vulnerable

Elements of Content

Nonfiction books are built chiefly on **exposition** with liberal doses of **anecdotes**, **examples**, **quotes** and **transitions** paced in balanced proportion throughout the narrative.

Exposition is the narrative of factual information. **Anecdotes** are the nonfiction equivalent of fictional action, which brings the reader closer to the material. For example, "Alexander the Great beat Darius on the plains of Issos" is simple exposition, but the anecdotal narration of how Alexander executed his battle campaign would be descriptive action, and thus give the reader more insight into the man's mind as well as the ambiance of the event and times.

Examples, such as the one used in the paragraph above, support or amplify the specific point being made. And though not all nonfiction authors employ quotes to bolster their claims, as Thomas H. Brennan attributed to Winston Churchill in *Writings on Writing* (Barnes & Noble Books, 1994) "Quotations when engraved upon the memory give you good thoughts."

Transitions, as noted above, are essential for moving from one discussion to another, and their lack is one of the most frequent and obvious mistakes new writers make. Without a smooth transition from one thought to another or one subject to another, anyone's writing can end up choppy and disjointed. If you simply cannot think of a statement or re-mark to tie one paragraph to the next or one idea to the next, use a subhead or break to a new chapter.

Step 4: Rewrite

Once you've structured and drafted the material, you'll have a viable manuscript with which to work. Believe it or not, the rest of the job is downhill.

In your second and third drafts, flesh out any ideas you did not sufficiently explain and correct any content discrep-ancies or continuity problems. If you are a practiced writer, you can also accomplish the bulk of the line edit. If you are a new author, make an additional pass to amend or tighten the slinky flow of each paragraph, chapter and book section and change where the chapters break, if necessary. Be sure you have adequate and appropriate transitions and subheadings. Eliminate or correct any focus or resolution inconsistencies, digressions, ambiguities, inconclusive or extraneous material. Add or expand examples or case histories, if necessary, and make sure they're focused for the point you want to make and correlate with the resolution or conclusions you offer.

The rest of the line edit consists of correcting any rhythm, pacing or color problems that leap out at you and converting passive voice to active, where appropriate. Either during or after the second draft, format the manuscript to conform to either submission or publishing standards.

Format

If you plan to submit your manuscript to a literary agent or traditional publisher, it should look as professional as pos-sible. Double-space all text. Leave a margin of at least 1-1.25" on both sides, the top and the bottom. Start your first page of each chapter one-third of the way down the page, or ap-proximately six double-spaced lines. Leave the right margin ragged (a.k.a. "left alignment") and avoid hyphenations, if possible. This is the era of computers, not typewriters, so use only one space between sentences, not two. Use a header on every page with the author's last name, the book title and the specific contents—Chapter 1, for example, or Proposal—on the left, and the page number on the right.

Use a conventional, 12-point, serif font comparable to Times Roman or Courier. Avoid script, cursive, italics or "clever" typefaces. Make sure the print is dark and un-smudged off a laser or desk-jet printer. Use white bond or at least good copy paper. Recycled paper may be great for the environment, but it's not necessarily the best material for a manuscript.

Did You Know?

Serifs are the small flags on the individual letters. San-serif type, such as Arial or Verdana, is larger than standard type, and begins to "swim" before the eyes after a few pages. Save these eye-catching fonts for titles, headings or any rare points that require special impact.

Always include a cover page with any submission longer than a short story. Caption the cover page with the author's name, address, phone number and fax or email contact in the upper left corner, single spaced. Include either the projected word count of the book or the actual count of the proposal in the upper right corner. Center the title approximately one-third of the way down the page, the subtitle one double space below the title and the author's name one double space below that. If you have one, include your agent's name, address and phone number, single spaced, in the lower right corner.

Author   Approx. 67,250 words
Street Address
City, State Zip
Phone Number
Email or Fax Contact

BOOK TITLE

SUB TITLE
Author

                                    Agent
                            Street Address
                            City, State Zip
                            Phone Number
                        Fax or Email Contact

Author//Title/Chapter   1

CHAPTER 1
    Leave a third of the page blank at the
beginning of every chapter, and indent the
first line of every paragraph. You can create
a "style" for this on most word-processing
programs. Do not justify the right margin.
    Be consistent with using periods at the
end of bulleted lists.

- Item one.
- Item two.

Or:

- Item one
- Item two

But not:

- Item one
- Item two.

6

Fiction

If you fancy yourself a novelist, you've probably had a story in mind for quite a while. You may even have written the manuscript or at least a first draft. Of that 81% of Americans who feel they have a book in them, probably at least half were talking about novels or children's stories. Even though the majority of books published every year are non-fiction, writing is dreaming and imagining, and that just naturally lends itself to creating fiction.

Fiction is significantly more intricate and frustrating than nonfiction. Perhaps the most difficult part of crafting a first novel involves coming to terms with two harsh realities: 1) a sequence of events is not a plot and 2) characters who do not expose themselves beyond their immediate actions within that plot are one-dimensional. Once again, the best way to avoid or correct these predicaments is to reduce the material down to its most basic elements of 1) research, 2) plot and character development, 3) the first draft, 4) rewrite and 5) format/editing.

Step 1: Research

Most first novels—indeed, many subsequent titles as well—are set in the author's hometown and lifetime. The scenes are played out in familiar rooms and outdoor locations and the characters are based on friends, relatives, coworkers or close acquaintances. Novelists tend to create autobiographies of one sort or another, consciously or not. Theoretically, everything a writer does in life will eventually end up on paper; hence, every book, trip or daily occurrence is not only "life experience" for an author, but potential research for a forthcoming book—an artistic reality, by the way, but not an acceptable excuse for income tax purposes. The IRS **will not** accept deductions for research trips and exclusive materials unless the experience contributed to a specific project that produced income.

If you want to use locations, characters, cultures, social circles or plot twists beyond your own experiences, you will need to immerse yourself personally in the ambiance and taste of those circumstances. Do not try to rely on other people's books to capture the spirit of blue-blood society, for example. Instead, attend a debutante's ball or wrangle an invitation to an exclusive country club. If experiences like these are not possible and you have no previous exposure to that particular social strata, reconsider your settings.

Some fiction does require conventional research. A story of international intrigue, for example, may be within your bounds of knowledge but still require airline routes, customs procedures or the precise location of certain landmarks or points of interest. That, too, is research. Before you write a story that takes place during a summer car trip between Dallas and Seattle, you need to replicate the journey at that time of year so you can include the details of road conditions and peculiarities, restaurants and truck stops, motels and side trips that help set the novel's location and feel. Research might also encompass following the international news or reading scholarly analyses of trends and events. Certainly any historical fiction must be researched for appropriate setting, clothing, biases, political attitudes and so forth.

Perhaps the most important form of fiction research, however, is one too many writers do not take seriously until faced with trying to flesh out their one-dimensional characters: people watching. Novelists need to absorb the human attributes and peculiarities that flesh out their characters by listening more than talking, reading more than writing and watching more than doing. Rather than simply stand in line at the grocery store, for example, observe, analyze and mentally record people's gestures, expressions and behaviors. We writers are notoriously untrustworthy in that respect; we may promise to never use our best friend in a book, but chances are that person's habit of pulling at her eyebrow or scrunching up his eyes or always expecting the worst will appear somewhere in our next book.

Unfortunately, many aspiring novelists have never taken notice of people beyond their small circle of influence. Their characters are all simply different aspects of themselves, and they have no stockpile of life and human observations from which they can create different subtleties, nuances, agendas or personality traits beyond their own perspectives. If they "walk a mile in someone else's shoes," they still only see what they would do, not how that other person might think or react. These are the novelists whose characters are critiqued as flat or one-dimensional, and whose stories are sequenced rather than plotted. Before you begin your novel, you must begin people watching—not interacting, just watching. Let your imagination come alive by writing stories *about* the people you watch, not for them.

Step 2A: Structure, a.k.a. Plot

The structure of a novel is its plot and subplots. Even a character-driven story needs a beginning/setup, conflict, story progression and a resolve and/or ending. Since any or all of those elements can change when your fully developed characters impact the action, character development must also be considered part of the structure process.

Creative-writing and novel-technique instructors are almost as numerous as the stars in the heavens, all with their own methods for developing plots and subplots. The following suggestions, therefore, are just two more possibilities to add to your collection.

Chart the Story

Create a plot/character map by repeatedly answering the question, "Then what happens?" Using a two-column table, note where the story begins in row one, column one. Answer "and then what happens?" in row two, column one. Next to it, in column two, list "why?" Continue listing what happens next and why it happens until you get to the ending, making sure that either the characters' reactions have an effect on the progress of the conflicts, obstacles and undeserved misfortune that occur during the story (character-driven), or that the incidents themselves affect the characters (plot-driven).

The upside to this method of plotting is that it creates a scene-by-scene map of the entire book, which clearly demonstrates how and why the protagonist undergoes an emotional change, resolves a significant problem or makes a life-changing decision by the end of the book. The downside is that it can lead to one-dimensional characters unless your "why?" answers address their personalities, perspectives and agendas. Suppose, for example, you have a scene in which a man goes to see his dying father in the hospital. Column one lists: **Sam goes to see father in hospital.** Column two, or "Why?" needs to be more than simply, **Because he's dying** or **To say goodbye,** both of which indicate you have little grasp of who your character is, or why he does what he does. On the other hand, **Out of respect** or **Because his mother expects him to** or **To make sure the bastard's really going to die this time** provides the kind of insight that helps make whatever comes next interesting and plausible.

Once you've got the entire story mapped out, go back and rearrange, add, subtract or modify as much as necessary until you have a full outline of your solid, compelling story. This will be the basis for writing your first draft, so make sure the characters' reactions are reasonable, the plot twists are plausible and any "holes" or inconsistencies are rectified before you start writing.

When you are backtracking through a completed manuscript, list the scenes in each chapter, simplify each description down to a blurb and then reduce to a single sentence or phrase. Eventually, you should have a long list of nothing but action, just as if you had created the map from scratch. Extract all the subplot aspects into a separate list; what remains is the primary story line. If it follows an actual plot, it will have a beginning/set-up, at least one if not a series of conflicts, a resolve and/or an ending. If the plot map is missing any of those crucial aspects, you will have to attempt to supply them. Exceptions abound, of course. Action/adventure books have been known to end with the resolve. Series fiction may finish with a teaser about the next title. Sci-fi is sometimes left purposely unresolved. You get the idea.

The typical sequence-of-events manuscript will lack specific conflicts, known in screen parlay as "undeserved misfortunes," that force the characters' hands and hence move the story forward. Remember, however, that books are not movies, and circumstances by themselves are not conflicts. Then again, characters can manipulate any given set of circumstances into trouble for other characters, or even for themselves, depending on their own attitudes/perspectives/biases.

Meet in the Middle

The Hollywood trick of jumping back and forth between the beginning and the end of the story only seems absurd until you try it. In fact, once you've plotted a story this way, you may never use any other method again. It's especially useful for trying to create a story from nothing more than a germ of an idea or a single scene.

Number a piece of paper from one to 15. Write a one-line blurb of where the story begins next to number one. Write the ending next to number 15. Go back to the top and write a blurb for what happens after the opening next to number two. Jump back to number 14 and write what happened just before the story ends. Continue bouncing from the top of the page to the bottom. After the story is complete, you can modify or add any sequences and character motivations.

This method is fast, easy and foolproof. Unfortunately, it is also shallow; those 15 scenes are just the highlights of the story. A lot of action and motivation must be filled in to complete the picture, but since the process takes only a few minutes, you can then use it as a starting point to create the entire plot map. In demonstration, let's create a basic boy/girl story. If this was playing out on an interactive disk, the lines would pop up from top to bottom, but since we're working with paper and ink, the font change indicates movement between the top of the page (italics) and the bottom (all caps) until they meet in the middle (shaded).

1: *Boy meets girl. We'll call the boy Bill and the girl Sandy.*

15: BILL KILLS THE MURDERER. WHAT MURDERER, YOU ASK? WHO KNOWS? AT THE END OF THE STORY, BILL IS GOING TO KILL A MURDERER.

2: *Bill's ex shows up. Whether she's an ex-wife or an ex-girlfriend does not matter right now.*

14: SANDY ESCAPES FROM THE MURDERER. IF BILL'S GOING TO KILL HIM, SANDY OUGHT TO GET AWAY FIRST, RIGHT?

3: *Sandy and Bill fight and break up. Remember, Bill's ex has just shown up, and all boy/girl stories have a "boy loses girl" aspect.*

13: THE MURDERER TORTURES SANDY, WHICH WOULD CERTAINLY MAKE HER WANT TO ESCAPE!

4: *Sandy goes to a nightclub and meets the murderer. Having just broken up with Bill, she's vulnerable, although she probably does not know the guy wants more than just a goodnight kiss.*

12: MURDERER KIDNAPS SANDY. WELL, DUH — HOW ELSE WOULD SHE GET TORTURED?

5: *Bill heads out to look for Sandy.*

11: BILL'S EX SICS THE MURDERER ON SANDY. YOU JUST KNEW SHE WASN'T A NICE PERSON. THE MURDERER

KNOWS, TOO; HE KILLS HER. NOBODY LIKES A TURN-COAT.

6: *Bill's ex follows him and brings him home to bed. He was out looking for Sandy, remember?*

10: BILL THROWS HIS EX OUT. ABOUT TIME, TOO, HUH?

7: *After kissing the murderer goodnight, Sandy finds Bill in bed with the ex.*

9: BILL TELLS HIS EX HE LOVES SANDY; SHE THREATENS TO MAKE HIM SORRY.

8: Devastated by Bill's infidelity, Sandy goes running out of the house.

Okay, the story has met in the middle. When you put it in order, here's how it reads:

1: Bill meets Sandy.

2: Bill's ex shows up.

3: Sandy and Bill fight and break up.

4: Sandy goes to a nightclub and meets murderer.

5: Bill heads out to look for Sandy.

6: Bill's ex follows Bill and brings him home to bed.

7: After kissing the murderer goodnight, Sandy finds Bill in bed with the ex.

8: Devastated by Bill's infidelity, Sandy goes running out of the house.

9: BILL TELLS HIS EX HE LOVES SANDY; SHE THREATENS TO MAKE HIM SORRY.

10: BILL THROWS HIS EX OUT.

11: BILL'S EX SICS THE MURDERER ON SANDY. MURDERER KILLS BILL'S EX.

12: MURDERER KIDNAPS SANDY.

13: MURDERER TORTURES SANDY.

14: SANDY ESCAPES FROM THE MURDERER.

15: BILL KILLS THE MURDERER.

As you can see, the result is a relatively simplistic story line, but with your vivid imagination and a good character study, you can develop it into a full plot.

Step 2B: Build Your Characters

> ## Did You Know?
> According to conventional literary wisdom, a writer has anywhere from six to thirty-six possible plots on which to base a novel. Yet, an infinite number of books have and will be written using those few basic story ideas. What makes one boy-meets-girl story different from every other boy-meets-girl story?
> Why, the boy and the girl, of course. Who are your boys and girls?

Characters are the crux of any novel. Films may focus on action or special effects, but books are peopled with…people. If you're a first-time novelist, you have undoubtedly visualized your plot, characters and stand-out scenes so many times that when someone says your characters are one-dimensional, you have no idea what that means or how to rectify the problem. Trying to "show, not tell," a phrase so bandied about it has become a cliché, seldom helps. Nor does including florid descriptions of the characters' hair, face, clothing or attitude, or inserting backstory or poignant snippets about the time Charlie lost his dog or Julia slept with her best friend's fiancé. Instead, you must consider changing what those main characters do, or how the new backstory, revamped hairstyles or sharp-toned dialogue may affect the way the plot unfolds.

Most new authors "see" their story line more clearly than the people in it, and put together a strong, plot-driven novel in which only those character aspects that pertain directly to the story need apply. In an action/adventure, for example, the characters' derring-do, or lack thereof, takes the forefront. If the work's theme is romance, the only thing on anyone's mind is love, attraction and/or sex. Nevertheless, to make the book work from a cold reader's perspective, the main character must undergo an emotional journey throughout the course of the book and arrive at the end a changed person. That is the whole point of a written piece of fiction.

Character-driven stories are those in which the primary characters' thoughts, feelings and reactions impact the plot, subplots, climax(es) and resolve of the book. This does not negate having a story in mind at the beginning of the book, but rather that the story may take turns or even have a different outcome than originally conceived. Authors sometimes argue about whether or not their characters can "take over" a story. Those who claim they do tend to write character-driven stories. Those who claim they don't either write plot-driven stories, or have mastered the art to such an extent that they have resolved every aspect of their work before they begin to write. Yes, such people most definitely do exist. But they're in the minority.

Take This Quick Test

Suppose the main character of your novel was of the opposite gender. Would the story change?

Suppose the main character had been sexually abused as a child. Would that alter the character's response to the story's various plot points?

Would it affect the outcome of your story line if your main character was politically conservative or liberal?

Would it make a difference if your main character had been brought up in a poor rural town or a middle-class, blue-collar neighborhood?

Imagine that one of the main character's parents had marched at Selma or hated Asians or had never voted or had committed suicide. Would the main character react any differently?

Does it matter if your main character ever served in the military or fought in a war or experienced death first-hand?

If you answered "no" to more than one or two of the above, you have a **plot-driven** story, where *what* happens is more important than *to whom* it happens. Ironically, the most common error in plot-driven novels is a <u>lack</u> of plot. When the characters take a backseat to the action, the story plays out in a flat sequence of events. In a sequence of events, one scene follows another simply due to author manipulation rather than character or subplot impact. The husband beats the wife because the author wants to show him as a meanie, not because he has any agenda or motive or compelling reason to beat her. There are few "Why?" answers in a sequence of events.

How Well Do You Know Your Characters?

Again, the methods of fleshing out characters or developing character studies are too numerous to count. The following exercise, therefore, is merely meant to nudge your imagination. It is by no means a complete character study, but it should get you thinking about everything your character(s) are or could be, and give you some ideas about perspective. Though none of these statements may make it into your manuscript, they may help you portray your characters as more real-to-life individuals.

~ ~ ~ ~ ~ ~ ~ ~ ~ ~ ~ ~ ~ ~ ~ ~ ~ ~

Hi, my name is: _____

My role in this story is

❏   Protagonist (main character)

❏   2nd Main character

❏   Secondary (supporting) character

❏   Minor character

I am a _____-year-old ❏ male ❏ female

I live in:

❏   a hovel   ❏   a small house

❑ a small apartment   ❑ a large house
❑ a large apartment   ❑ a mansion
❑ a condo   ❑ on an estate

other _____

With: _____

My occupation is: _____

My academic level is: _____

My socioeconomic status is:

❑ dirt poor   ❑ upper-middle class
❑ poor   ❑ moderately wealthy
❑ working poor   ❑ very wealthy
❑ Lower-middle class   ❑ filthy rich
❑ middle class   ❑ multi-millionaire
❑ middle-middle class   ❑ rich beyond the dreams of
                             avarice

My race/nationality is: _____

At the beginning of the book, my main concern in life is: ____

Throughout the book, I encounter a challenge to my:

❑ attitudes   ❑ emotional stability
❑ biases   ❑ sense of security or safety
❑ self-perceptions   ❑ emotional attachments
❑ abilities   ❑ other: _____

By the end of the book, I have changed my:

❑ attitudes   ❑ emotional stability
❑ biases   ❑ sense of security or safety
❑ self-perceptions   ❑ emotional attachments
❑ abilities   ❑ other: _____

That change affects how I:
- ❑ work
- ❑ vote
- ❑ handle crises
- ❑ deal with life
- ❑ deal with my family
- ❑ feel about myself
- ❑ relate to God
- ❑ other:_____

At the end of the book, my main concern in life is: _____

I think of myself as:
- ❑ intellectually superior
- ❑ smarter than most, not as smart as others
- ❑ of average intelligence
- ❑ not too bright
- ❑ uh, what was the question again?

My favorite description of myself is: _____

My most ardent admirer describes me as: _____

My worst enemy describes me as: _____

When I talk to someone, I tend to:
- ❑ look around the room
- ❑ maintain eye contact
- ❑ alternate between eye contact and glancing around
- ❑ leave my hands at rest
- ❑ crack my knuckles
- ❑ play with my fingers or rings
- ❑ gesture
- ❑ drum my fingers
- ❑ touch the other person's hand or arm
- ❑ run my hands through my hair
- ❑ wring my hands
- ❑ touch my chin, mouth, clothes, etc.
- ❑ other _____

I talk ❑ quickly ❑ slowly ❑ at a moderate pace.

I ❑ do ❑ do not have an accent. (type) _____

My laugh is:
- ❏ loud
- ❏ soft
- ❏ a giggle
- ❏ a snort
- ❏ a honk
- ❏ a mixture of sounds

I walk ❏ quickly ❏ slowly ❏ at a moderate speed. When no one is looking, I:
- ❏ skip
- ❏ shuffle
- ❏ run
- ❏ weave
- ❏ wander
- ❏ change my pace
- ❏ do not change my walk

I consider myself a:
- ❏ Passive person
- ❏ Controlled person
- ❏ Violent person

When I am angry, I:
- ❏ yell
- ❏ snarl
- ❏ become abusive
- ❏ keep quiet
- ❏ watch others
- ❏ plot revenge

I show my anger with:
- ❏ my tone of voice
- ❏ my gestures
- ❏ my body language
- ❏ my facial expression
- ❏ I never show anger

I show impatience with:
- ❏ my tone of voice
- ❏ my gestures
- ❏ my body language
- ❏ my facial expression
- ❏ I never show impatience

I show happiness with:
- ❏ my tone of voice
- ❏ my gestures
- ❏ my facial expression
- ❏ I never show happiness

❏ my body language

I show embarrassment with:

❏ my tone of voice   ❏ my facial expression
❏ my gestures   ❏ my body language
❏ I never show embarrassment

I show love with:

❏ my tone of voice   ❏ my facial expression
❏ my gestures   ❏ I never show love
❏ my body language

The gesture I use most is: _____

The gesture I wish I could stop using is: _____

My driving is usually:

❏ aggressive   ❏ timid
❏ defensive   ❏ I don't drive

When I'm stressed I drive ❏ worse ❏ more cautiously ❏ the same

The Truth Is ...

I brush my teeth twice a day

    ❏ Always ❏ Sometimes ❏ Never

I shower/bathe daily

    ❏ Always ❏ Sometimes ❏ Never

I maintain a healthy diet

    ❏ Always ❏ Sometimes ❏ Never

I eat breakfast

    ❏ Always ❏ Sometimes ❏ Never

I pay bills promptly

    ❏ Always ❏ Sometimes ❏ Never

I open my mail immediately

  ❑ Always   ❑ Sometimes   ❑ Never

I borrow money

  ❑ Always   ❑ Sometimes   ❑ Never

I loan money

  ❑ Always   ❑ Sometimes   ❑ Never

I call my mother regularly

  ❑ Always   ❑ Sometimes   ❑ Never

I cheat on my spouse

  ❑ Always   ❑ Sometimes   ❑ Never

I vote in national elections

  ❑ Always   ❑ Sometimes   ❑ Never

I do my own/others' laundry

  ❑ Always   ❑ Sometimes   ❑ Never

I cook my own/others' meals

  ❑ Always   ❑ Sometimes   ❑ Never

I make my bed

  ❑ Always   ❑ Sometimes   ❑ Never

I go to religious services

  ❑ Always   ❑ Sometimes   ❑ Never

I grew up with: _____

My parents ❑ are ❑ are not divorced.

My mother ❑ is ❑ is not alive.

  She died when I was _____ years old.
  I ❑ did ❑ did not grow up with her.
  I am ❑ just like ❑ sometimes like ❑ not at all like her.
  I have always _____ her:
  ❑ Loved   ❑ Feared
  ❑ Admired   ❑ Resented

❏ Respected   ❏ Hated, loathed, and despised

The thing I always remember about her is: _____

My father is ❏ alive ❏ dead.

He died when I was _____ years old.

I ❏ did ❏ did not grow up with him.

I am ❏ just like ❏ sometimes like ❏ not at all like him.

I have always _____ him:

❏ Loved   ❏ Feared

❏ Admired   ❏ Resented

❏ Respected   ❏ Hated, loathed, and despised

The thing I always remember most about him is:

_____

I have _____ older brothers and _____ younger brothers

I have _____ older sisters and _____ younger sisters

The best way(s) to describe my family is:

❏ close   ❏ loud

❏ distant   ❏ quiet

❏ estranged   ❏ comfortable

❏ nonexistent   ❏ uncomfortable

❏ loving   ❏ passive

❏ hateful   ❏ aggressive

❏ fun   ❏ passive-aggressive

❏ melancholy   ❏ Ozzie & Harriet normal

❏ easygoing   ❏ dysfunctional

❏ strict   ❏ happy

❏ religious   ❏ charitable

❏ irreverent   ❏ snobbish

❏ Other:

My most vivid family memory is: _____

~ ~ ~ ~ ~ ~ ~ ~ ~ ~ ~ ~ ~ ~ ~ ~ ~ ~ ~

Again, the above is just a beginning. To further explore your characters, create their educational background, even if it does not apply to the story, and think about their first romantic experience, their sexual proclivities, their biases and gullibilities, their agendas in life in general and in the story in particular. Take them out of the story altogether, and place them in other situations to see how they act, think and feel. If your main character was played by Humphrey Bogart or Ingrid Bergman, how would the last scene of Casablanca play out? How would your character deal with being unjustly arrested, called in front of a Senate investigating committee, or winning the lottery? Suppose a parent, sibling or best friend died unexpectedly in the middle of your story—how would your character handle it? Think outside your story, and you'll develop a better feel for your character in the story.

Step 3: The First Draft

Now that you've got your story plotted and your characters developed, narrate each map or scene blurb into a full scene, keeping those character traits firmly in mind. Again, remember the advantage of a first draft: it **will** be rewritten, so don't worry about whether you are using passive voice, telling rather than showing, employing sufficient dialogue or punctuating your sentences correctly. Just write out the entire story from beginning to end, developing character motivation, scenic description and so forth in whatever form is most comfortable for you. If you have used any of the methods above, you should not have a problem with Writer's Block.

Elements of Content

Novels employ **action, dialogue, description** and **exposition** to reveal the characters who weave through their plots.

Action, or physical activity, can be as simple as a character coughing or as complex as the execution of a military tactic. In the narrow sense, action is the physical movement of a character as he gives a speech, flicks a cigarette butt into the ashtray, clears his throat, darts his eyes around the room. In the broader sense, action might refer to an entire scene that moves the story forward, such as a race to the hospital complete with dialogue, description, and narration. Action is narrated, and should be presented from a consistent point of view.

Dialogue is quoted conversational material; one person speaks to another aloud. Internal thoughts are not considered dialogue since they are never verbalized, so they are either italicized or attributed—not both—but not bracketed with quotation marks.

> "I think he's lying," she said.
> He's lying, she thought.
> She narrowed her eyes. *Liar.*

Description is the device used to familiarize the reader with a setting, a character's attire or an object of note. Reveal your descriptions via active narration that provides color for the setting or person, rather than as an insert that stops the flow of the story.

Exposition moves the story forward, provides background information or in any other way "tells" what is going on until the next action or dialogue sequence.

Background provides depth to a character, assertion or situation, and fills the reader in on what came before, thereby establishing a specific perspective for what is happening now. Background can be revealed through dialogue or narration, but should never simply be inserted in long exposition form that stops the flow of the story or stuffed into pseudo dialogue.

Character refers to the personality traits that distinguish the people in the story from each other and make them interesting. Characters not only require the mechanical device of point of view, they should also each have their own, individual perspectives. Any given event, for example, will be viewed differently by each character involved since, even if they agree on what happened, the meaning and effect of the event will be different to each individual's life.

Setting, like action, has both a narrow and broad meaning. In the former sense, setting refers to the specific location where a scene is played out—the boardroom of a major corporation, for instance. In the latter sense, the setting of New York City, circa 1936, establishes a tone and perspective for the look of that boardroom, the attitudes and clothes of the characters, the economic and political atmosphere and so forth.

A **hiatus** is an unseen or unused gap in time, and can be achieved through transitional descriptions or remarks that let the reader know time has passed: As the sun rose the next morning ... or She looked at her watch. 4:30 already! Hiatus can also be accomplished physically by leaving two double spaces between appropriate paragraphs.

Segues, the fiction version of transitions, can be used when changing from one point of view to another, to help move the narrative from present time to flashback and back again and to provide a "set up" that makes the reader want to turn the page at the end of the chapter. If you cannot segue, use a hiatus or chapter break.

Pacing is an abstract element that refers to the speed and proportion of prose as well as the plot's forward movement. The type of story generally dictates the desired pace of the book. Fast-paced mystery and horror stories, for example, push the reader along through suspense-laden action to a startling climax. A thoughtful exploration of a mid-life crisis, on the other hand, would read better at a slower, more introspective pace.

Did You Know?

Pacing is part of the art, not the craft of writing. Craft can be studied and taught. Art is instinctive, and must be developed.

Points to Ponder

The line between craft and art begins to blur once ideas start to expand on paper. Although writers customarily know what they want to say and how they want it to be said, certain literary practices can aid in getting those ideas across to the reader in common-usage or easily recognizable form. Radicalism in content can transform apathy into activism; radicalism in format, on the other hand, merely confuses the reader. Certain principles and techniques are considered standard practice. Excitement, suspense, fear, thrill and lust, for example, are heightened by fast-paced movement, sharp images and clean action.

Point of view (POV) and **perspective** are not the same thing. **POV** refers to who is speaking and what that person is thinking or feeling. Perspective refers to the reason behind those thoughts, actions and feelings. Even if all your characters speak alike, they should not all react or think alike. A character's perspective both directs and depends on his agenda, biases, background and so forth, and is developed as part of the character study. In simple terms, POV refers to who is holding the camera; perspective refers to the "Why?" aspect of the character in whose POV the story is being told.

While you may **describe** your major characters' appearance, **reveal** their perspectives, agendas, biases, and so forth over the course of the book in their words, actions and reactions rather than in a matter of a few paragraphs or pages.

Describe minor characters briefly at the point of their entry into the story.

Focus in on **panoramic** scene descriptions of settings or locations to the details that make a reader feel present at the site. A majestic canyon wall, for example, or the sun's purple haze setting behind billowy white clouds gives a feel for the time and place, but the reader will get a feel of being on a cliff from the stones that rattle over the edge as the character picks his way forward.

Author intrusion is the practice of revealing to the audience something the POV character does not know. For example:

> Little did Aubry know how much that amulet would mean to her later.

If Aubry did not know at this point, neither should the reader. Along the same lines, if a husband and wife are on the brink of divorce and can barely stand to look at each other, describing his stud attributes or her head-turning beauty is author intrusive, since neither of them would be thinking in those terms at this point.

Fact stuffing is usually disguised as dialogue that fills the reader in on background, personality and so forth:

> "John, I know you've been under a lot of pressure lately. Your wife's been sick and your little boy is having trouble in school. Sure, you've been with the company for several years now, but I can tell you're a little bitter about losing that promotion you were in line for last month...."

Adverbs are a source of debate, especially when used to modify "said" during dialogue. The accepted format of using "he said" for all dialogue can become boring, although the attribution tends to be invisible. Substitutions such as "he sneered" or "he whimpered" can easily get out of hand. One school of thought believes any attempt to modify "said," such as "he said fiercely" or "he said quietly," detracts from the force of the dialogue. Another group believes dialogue should be written in such a way that no attribution is ever necessary. You could drive yourself nuts trying to conform to all these hard-and-fast "rules" that are usually delivered with the voice of authority but are really nothing more than strongly held opinions. Do yourself a favor; use a combination of all four, applying whichever one seems most appropriate for each passage. There are only two "rules" in fiction: 1) it must be compelling and 2) it must be plausible within itself. Beyond that, if it works, it works.

All people fight an **internal battle** in order to display the characteristics for which they are known, and you need to demonstrate that battle if you're going to have your characters change from their normal behavior. The methodical, painstakingly accurate accountant who experiences a life crisis and suddenly finds himself jumping to conclusions or taking uncalculated risks, for example, would be acting out of character unless you'd shown how his sense of reality had been challenged. Don't change the story line; alter his persona.

No human being is 100% good nor 100% evil. "Perfect" individuals are shallow, one-dimensional **caricatures**, best left where they belong—on TV, in the comics and on the film screen. Characterization is created through **contradiction**—through dealing with the hypocrisy of life and one's internal conflicts. An individual with no internal conflicts would be … well … inhuman.

Step 4: Rewrite as Necessary

Once you have finished the first draft, do a second pass to flesh out the scenes, deepen the characterizations and convert static dialogue into conversation and "tell" into "show," where appropriate. Create the chapter cliffhangers or segues that compel the reader to turn the page, and correct any minor inconsistencies or implausibilities. Revise your chapter breaks and hiatuses, if necessary, and eliminate any remaining POV problems.

Most first-time novelists—and many well-established ones, for that matter—rewrite their novels three or five or twelve times, fleshing out characters, altering scenes, adjusting plots and correcting rhythm, pacing, color, continuity errors, inconsistencies and so forth. In fact, if you are like most educated writers, you will continue to tweak your novel until it says exactly what you want it to say, exactly the way you want it said. As John Dos Passos, author of the trilogy *U.S.A.*, said, "I usually write to a point where the work is getting worse rather than better."

Show and Tell Simplified

Clichés may be trite, but usually only because they are true. You can reveal the contents of a canvas in two ways: describe the work, or allow your readers to experience it themselves: show or tell. Even though every individual who has ever picked up a book or taken a class on writing knows the difference between these two approaches and is probably bored to death thinking about them, most will include an excessive amount of exposition in their work, thereby "telling" rather than "showing."

What, exactly, is "showing?" It's merely a writing technique that allows readers to feel present in the scene, and *decide for themselves* what the POV character is feeling or experiencing. Unlike passive vs. active voice, which is an editing matter, "show, not tell" is addressed in the rewriting stage.

An inordinate number of aspiring authors simply do not understand the ramifications of this concept, possibly because the phrase "show, not tell" has been reiterated to the point of inanity. Perhaps another way to interpret the idea, therefore, is to think of showing as "opening up" the material; taking a bit of description or thought or attitude and creating a scene or piece of action that lets the reader experience, rather than simply observe the story.

Another way to grasp the difference is to think of "show" as interactive writing, in which the reader responds to the scene or description on more than a visual or intellectual level. Physical activity plus emotional response, for example, lets the reader experience the sensation along with the character. Ergo, while "He disgusted her," is no more interactive than, "She hated him," "Every time he touched her hand, her skin crawled," is, because it lets the reader experience what the character experiences by combining physical activity with emotional response. Consider the following.

The box was heavy. He put it on the table.

vs.

The box seemed to pull back as he dragged it across the room. Rocking it, he stuck one foot under a corner, leaving just enough room for his fingers to get a grip. As he strained to lift it onto the table, he felt a sharp ping in his lower back.

Musta been heavy, huh?

To show a sharp, vibrant image, use words that provoke an emotion. Writers often interpret this to mean "use a lot of adjectives or adverbs," an approach that leads, once again, to description rather than experience. The emotions of fear, bravery, passion, honesty, love, charity, warmth, pathos, earthiness, pride and so on, are provoked through an active appeal to the physical senses of sight, sound, taste, touch and smell. Hence, "He was afraid to run his forefinger around the rim of the vase for fear it would crack under the slightest pressure," is a far more visceral image than, "The vase was thin and delicate."

Senses Don't Necessarily Show

Every fiction writer knows that the way to involve the reader in his prose is to use the five senses: sight, sound, touch, taste and smell. But human beings have more senses than those. Think about how you can wake up from a dead sleep and *know* someone else is in the house. Or the feeling you get the first time you meet someone extraordinary. Or the way life goes into slow motion or you feel "removed" when you hear horrifying news. You actually have dozens of senses you can use to bring your writing to life. Too often, however, aspiring authors actually write the sense, rather than evoke it.

> **She could hear the horses coming in the distance.**

The reader now knows the character can hear, and that horses are in the vicinity, which may be all you want to say. To evoke an emotional response with the character's sensation, however, let him actually hear what the character hears:

> **The distant rumble grew louder and more clear by the minute, finally sharpening into pounding hoofs.**

In this age of flash images, sound-byte news and streaming web videos, it's easy to forget that books were the first form of interactive entertainment. If you "tell" the tale, your readers will never experience the joy of being "inside" the story. While you needn't concern yourself with this technique during the initial draft, "telling" should be converted to "showing" during the rewrite process via dialogue, thought, developmental description and physical action and reaction.

Recognizing "Tell"

Telling can be either passive or active and may, indeed, arouse an emotional response, but seldom provides any insight into character or story. Telling is easily spotted by these devices:

Passive emotions, which occur when a line states an emotional response as if it was a mere fact: "he got angry" or "she was frightened." This is classic telling.

Passive senses, which are easily recognizable by the inclusion of the sense: she felt, he heard, she smelled, he saw. The reader is totally removed from what is being felt, heard, smelled or seen.

Flat exposition, such as, "Two young men discussed their dates the night before as they jogged along the flower-lined sidewalk under a clear blue sky." We know they were having a discussion, but we don't know what was said; it's almost as if the author is challenging the reader to guess the conversation's content. The show version might read:

> John veered to avoid the snapdragons hanging over the edge of the sidewalk. "Did you take Joanne to see that movie last night?"
>
> "Yeah," Bob grinned. "But it stunk, just like you said it would."

Excessive anthropomorphizing, wherein a breeze drifts across the clouds, wafts through the leaves, sweeps over the meadow, trips along the road and sings in the rafters, but has no effect whatsoever on either the story or the characters: "The car remained silent and motionless while traffic grew impacted. Vehicles struggled to fight their way around the luxurious sedan and for a time, pedestrians witnessed how empty fury could be vented at a mute, uncaring obstacle." This would work, of course, if the book was a graphic novel—the modern incarnation of a comic book—about a car that wants to be a real boy. In a story about industrial espionage, it is simply over the top.

Gushing on the page. For example, "She could not stand him. Not in the slightest bit. In her eyes, the man was nothing but a slimeball, a low-life sleaze that had oozed out of the sewer. The slick façade, the over-friendly manner, the oily smile—they were nothing but just that, she knew: a façade. Nothing but frilly window-dressing that in no way concealed, at least to her, the thick layer of slime beneath." A vivid description, without a doubt, but all exposition, and so much of it, you want to yell, "I get the message!" halfway through.

Bleeding on the page, as in, "She covered her mouth with her hand. She couldn't take any more. How could God have abandoned her like this? She'd always been taught to trust in His love. Where was He now? Now, when she needed Him more than ever!" Oh, anguish! Oh, angst! Oh, get over it.

Explaining what has been shown: "He curled his lip and slowly dragged his fingers down the front of her dress, transferring the bloody mess back to its original owner. He felt disgusted." Ya think?

Recognizing "Show"

Showing has a far greater impact on the story, the characters or the reader's understanding of those characters, whether written in active or passive voice. For example, nowhere in, "People hurried around him breathing like steam locomotives wrapped in long overcoats, hands stuffed in pockets, faces red, noses runny," does the author mention that the weather is cold, but the reader has no problem recognizing that fact by the way the characters are acting.

Here's another example of active showing: "I steered my pallet jack down the cereal aisle, slammed to a stop in front of the Rice Krispies, scanned my order list again and grimaced. I needed a full pallet's worth, and somebody had already broken up the load. I jumped down from the saddle and started slinging cases of cereal on top of my already 4-foot-high pile." The "tell" version might have read simply, "I started filling the orders on my list."

Showing can also be passive. Consider this initial description of the main character from Marian Thurm's *The Clairvoyant* (Harper Paperbacks, 1999): "He looked ordinary enough, like a man who earned his living in any one of the usual ways—in his corduroy pants, denim shirt and dark knit tie, he might have been a teacher, a photographer, a gallery owner. His hair, just long enough for a tiny ponytail, was perfectly straight, a mix of blond and gray that kept people guessing about his age. In spite of his beakish nose, he had the sort of strong, almost handsome face that women found appealing." The reader gets a picture of the character's personality and temperament as well as appearance, despite a lack of action and a succession of "to be" verbs.

Showing is not about manipulating "ly" modifiers or long-winded adjectives, but rather about painting a verbal picture so the <u>reader</u> can decide what the character is thinking, feeling, doing or trying to portray. If "Her heart pounded against her breastbone..." for instance, the character could be frightened, panicked, excited or simply out of shape. If the rest of sentence read, "...as her lover gently stroked the inside of her thigh," do we really need to be **told** why her heart is pounding?

7
Editing

Like the writing process, editing is a multi-layered procedure. It actually begins during the rewrite, when you adjust and modify as you restructure and revamp, and continues until you have corrected the last typographical error in the polished manuscript. Only then is the project "good enough" for submission to a publisher or literary agent.

Most aspiring authors can benefit from a third-party professional line edit—many, however, are not prepared to handle the results. Writers who send off a manuscript (along with a check and a prayer) in answer to faceless ads are often horrified at the state of its return. They expect a few minor grammar and punctuation notations, and get, instead, page after page of red-inked changes to almost every sentence along with margins full of advisory comments and notes about rewriting this or rethinking that. Too often, the response to "all that red" is to disregard the edit or, just as useless, get angry with the editor.

Try to look upon any third-party edit as a learning experience—not of the bias of the third party, which may be your first inclination, but of the subtle changes that can be made to improve and tighten your manuscript. Line edits are not rejections, indictments or comments on your inherent talent and abilities as a writer, but simply attempts to improve a written piece of work—nothing more.

A line edit performed by an objective, competent reader will make only those modifications necessary for clear and intelligible communication. If it also helps you learn how to communicate more succinctly the next time you put pen to paper, so much the better. If it only causes your ulcer to burn, don't quit your day job.

What to Look for in a Professional

Certainly it matters who performs the third-party edit. A friend who has little more experience than you can actually do more damage than good. The newer the writer, the more experienced the editor must be.

Because a writer's first third-party line-edit can be so highly traumatic, you must find an editor you can both respect and trust on a personal level. Remember to look for an <u>editor</u>, not just a writer, and plan to meet the individual, at least by phone. Email is not necessarily a good avenue for determining whether two people are artistically compatible.

> For referral to a Professional Book Writer™ or experienced ghost or editor, call 1-800-641-3936 or go to www.wambtac.com

Referrals are the best way to go, if at all possible. Before you hand over your manuscript, discuss the condition of the book as well as what you can expect. Look for someone who tends to see the value of any writer's voice, rather than one who tends toward making all voices generic. Ask for references, if possible.

While no editor can predict how many changes will be necessary or what the cost of those changes will be prior to an initial reading—and those who try should be considered suspect—professionals can explain what kinds of problems they will search for, as well as the extent to which they can handle those problems: **superficially**, which will leave the decision of how to correct a given problem to you; **moderately**, which will provide a structure or set of suggestions for you to modify; or **thoroughly**, which, for the inexperienced author, may result in the equivalent of a rewrite. These levels are sometimes referred to respectively as evaluation or critique, self-editing guidelines, and line editing or rewrite. With each successive degree of edit, expect the time and effort required to do the job as well as the subsequent cost to increase.

Nonfiction writers need to choose an editor somewhat familiar with their given field, at least insofar as recognizing appropriate terms or "buzz words." Fiction writers would do well to work with editors who have experience in their particular genre. These precautions may seem absurdly obvious, but in the heat of developing a book and searching for experienced help or guidance, simple matters are the ones most often forgotten, overlooked or ignored.

Pitfalls of Self-Editing

Because writing is such a personal, isolated and emotional endeavor, trying to disconnect from your own words is without question the hardest task you will ever face. Few writers can ever fully achieve true objectivity about their own work— or anyone else's, for that matter. In a strictly subjective medium, honesty, too, is subjective. The entire point of putting your thoughts on paper is, after all, to elicit an emotional reaction of one sort or another from an unknown reader, even if that emotion is only to agree with and implement, for example, a technical plan.

While you can edit your work to a point, the only way to be sure you are communicating with anyone other than yourself is for someone else to read it. Preferably, that means a "cold" reader; i.e., someone not connected to you or your work in any way. In almost all cases (and certainly if you are a novice), you would be better off hearing about your mistakes from a freelance editor, whose job is to strengthen your manuscript, than from an acquisitions editor, whose job is merely to accept or reject it.

That said, you do want to hold off on hiring an editor until you have completely finished rewriting and corrected the more obvious problems of passive voice, telling (not showing), dangling participles, word choice and so forth.

Did You know?

Some authors who fear their ideas might be stolen won't even hire their own editors. Yet, professional, experienced editors who apprenticed to senior editors are least likely to take another's ideas... The real challenge in hiring an editor is to distinguish the pro from those who claim to be, such as:

- the moonlighter, whose day job comes first
- the secretary, who's good at fixing the boss' correspondence
- the volunteer, who's applauded for producing the church bulletin or organizational newsletter
- the desktop publisher, who relies on grammar checkers and spell-checks
- the writer, who's secretly waiting to be published
- the English major, who thinks, 'What more do I need to know?"

Chris Roerden, award-winning senior book editor
<http://www.marketSavvyBookEditing.com>

The Editing Process

Editing comes in three flavors: line, copy and proof, depending upon the depth of correction. The only time these distinctions are important is when an outside party gets involved and needs to fix a price. Otherwise, the process comes down to a series of corrections, with the divisions noted below less distinct in reality than in theory:

Text order and flow (line)

Point-of-view continuity and transitions (line)

Rhythm, pacing, color (line)

Active vs. passive voice (line and copy)

Word usage vs. technical definition (copy)

Syntax (copy)

Spelling (copy and proof)

Typographical errors (proof)

Text Order and Flow

In a typical first draft presented by an aspiring author as a finished manuscript, sentences, paragraphs or even whole blocks of information, description or action may be out of sequence for the cold reader. This usually leads to redundancy or verbosity, both of which can be corrected simply by rearranging the material into the proper order. Consider this rather simplistic example:

> In a typical first draft presented by an aspiring author as a finished manuscript, redundancy and verbosity often need to be corrected. Sometimes, sentences, paragraphs or even whole blocks of information are found to be out of sequence. This has to be corrected, because it could lead to making the same point over and over, so it must be put back into the proper order.

By rearranging the above paragraph into proper order and deleting the extraneous phrases (as shown in the opening paragraph of this subsection), the paragraph conveys its message in a smoothly flowing sequence. This kind of correction should be taken care of during the first line-editing pass.

Point-of-View Continuity and Transitions

As noted above, **point of view** (POV) refers to whose mind is being read, whose thoughts overheard. Pov can change from chapter to chapter by refocusing the reader's attention to observe through the eyes of a different character. In a historical nonfiction, for example, the events contained in each chapter may be related from the consensual viewpoint of the era. In a novel, the first chapter might be told from the protagonist's point of view, the second from his adversary's and so on.

According to traditional creative-writing "rules," a novel should maintain one POV throughout an entire chapter, if not the entire book. Newer modifications allowed POV changes between hiatus points. In commercial fiction, however, **no such rules have ever existed** beyond the practicality of not changing POV so often as to confuse or annoy the reader. Problems only arise when aspiring authors change POV without realizing it, or without knowing exactly how to avoid it. Suppose we are in Karen's POV during this interchange:

> "Damn it!" Karen shouted. "I told you I wanted to read it before you shredded it!"
>
> "And I said I'd already taken care of it," Larry answered calmly, ignoring her outburst.

"Ignoring her outburst" is a conscious act, which means we have switched to Larry's POV, intentionally or not. To compound the problem, the phrase also unnecessarily "tells" what Larry has already shown by his tone of voice. To keep the conversation in Karen's POV, end the sentence at "answered calmly," or change the conscious act into one Karen can perceive:

> Larry shrugged. "And I said I'd already taken care of it. Have you seen the Portnif file? I've been looking for it all morning."

Karen's outburst has been effectively ignored without having changed into Larry's POV. Again, these changes are handled in the line edit.

Rhythm, Pacing, Color

Many writers believe these intangibles rightly belong in the writing/rewriting phase—and they are correct. However, since the **art** of writing—of which rhythm, pacing and color are intrinsic parts—cannot be taught, you need an editor with good instincts and an eye for linguistic flavor. If your material lacks color, pacing or rhythm, look for a line editor. Copy editors may flatten or "genericize" your unique prose with academic, style-guide or overly subjective revisions.

Active vs. Passive Voice

As much as passive voice is a highly touted transgression, make sure you work with an editor who knows how to tread lightly. After all, what is passive voice? In traditional academia, "passive" refers specifically to the "to be" verb in all its tenses: it is, it was, it will be, it had been, it can be, it might have been and so forth. In contemporary application, passive also refers to the kind of gobbledygook writing for which the government, as one example, is famous.

> "The copyright law of the United States governs the making of reproductions of copyrighted material."

Even without using the "to be verb," the above is so laden with prepositional phrases, superfluous articles and unnecessary gerunds that it defies communication. Removing some, albeit not all of the passive elements creates a more easily understood statement—which, of course, would be intolerable for most federal bureaucrats:

> "The United States' copyright law governs the reproduction of copyrighted material."

MS Word's Grammar Check notwithstanding, passive voice can be the most powerful way to express an idea. Consider one of the most famous opening lines in literature from Charles Dickens' *A Tale of Two Cities*:

> "It was the best of times, it was the worst of times."

Could you possibly convert that statement into active prose without totally diluting its impact and power?

> "The people enjoyed both good and bad times."

I don't think so. How about this opening line from George Orwell's *1984*:

> "It was a bright cold day in April, and the clocks were striking thirteen."

Or this more contemporary passive opening from John Grisham's *The Client*:

> "Mark was eleven and had been smoking on and off for two years."

Many otherwise excellent scribes and promising authors drive themselves crazy trying to eliminate passive voice at all costs. This pursuit is often not only unnecessary, but also counterproductive—she wrote passively.

Word Usage vs. Technical Definition

As noted earlier, some authors attempt to heighten their prose with "impressive" words. Here's a classic example:

> Her broad nose proudly stood between high cheek bones luminescing her doe brown eyes.

The technical definition of the noun luminescence is "production of light without heat, as in florescence" or "the light so produced" (*The American Heritage Dictionary, 4th Edition*, Houghton Mifflin 2001). The adjective luminescent, then, would indicate something that shines or glows without giving off heat. While the author probably meant the character had shining or sparkling doe-brown eyes, the line as written actually indicates that her nose made her eyes light up, an interesting but somewhat disturbing image. Still, she apparently wanted to infuse her writing with a scholarly tone rather than communicate simply, so a careful, non-generic editor would correct this line to something like:

> Her broad nose stood proudly between her high cheekbones and luminescent doe-brown eyes.

Here's an even better example of usage vs. technical definition:

> I was sadistically controlled by a behavior I had never felt before.

This sentence has a couple of problems. For one thing, a behavior cannot "sadistically control" since *sadistic* means "to take delight in cruelty" and a behavior has no capacity for that or any other emotion. Then again, people do not *feel* behavior, they...behave. Even transposing *sadistically* with *controlled* doesn't work, because behavior does not control a character, the character controls (or does not control) his behavior. Out of context, we can only guess at the correct phrasing, of course, but to correct the **usage,** we could guess that the author meant either:

I had never felt so sadistic before

or

I had never behaved so sadistically before

and edit from there.

When you tap into your dictionary, word-processor's synonym list or desk-size thesaurus, double-check your new term's form, actual meaning and appropriate usage. Otherwise, you might find the words you choose are not quite as efficacious (i.e., effective) as you would like.

Syntax

Strictly speaking, syntax involves making sure each individual sentence reads smoothly and coherently, and, as such, is the primary function of copy editing. From the traditional viewpoint, a sentence must be self-contained to be understandable, which means it must make sense as a statement when taken out of context, even if the full meaning is reliant on the statements made before or after. For example, "He bought it at a store" may leave the reader wondering who "he" and "it" is, but still conveys a complete thought. By way of contrast, the same is not true of the fragment, "Because of what he said."

The structure that allows a thought to be readily understood is called grammar. "Oh, no, not grammar!" you cry. Now, don't panic—grammar is not really a hodgepodge of rules set up merely to confound schoolchildren. It's actually a systematic description of how language works. Think of it in terms of a mechanical device. An automobile engine must be assembled in the proper order with all parts connected correctly or the car will not run. A sentence works the same way. Consider the following example:

While entering the room, a lamp fell off the table.

As it reads, the statement is utter nonsense: a lamp fell off the table while it entered the room. The writer's true intention is hidden because the sentence does not work, much the same way an engine whose parts have been assembled in the wrong order would not work. A more logical structure would include the appropriate pronoun:

As **he** entered the room, a lamp fell off the table.

Since the purpose of writing is to communicate, a sentence that leaves the reader confused has failed in its primary goal. Grammar, therefore, is merely a set of guidelines that allows the written word to communicate without ambiguity, confusion or comprehension difficulty, and the following is simply a catalog of grammatical elements for easy reference.

Devices

Sentences are words grouped into meaningful combinations by use of grammatical devices such as word order, function words, inflections, and the mechanical device of punctuation. A change in one of these devices, such as **word order**, causes a change in the sentence's meaning:

The teacher said the student was a genius.
The student said the teacher was a genius.

Function words, also known as **articles** and **connective words** —the, and, a, but, in, to, at, because and while—express relationships among other words to, once again, change sentence meanings. Some changes are subtle:

She was frightened in the dark.
She was frightened at the dark.

Others are more distinct:

They made a poor meal.
They made the poor a meal.

Inflections are the pitch your voice takes when reading a sentence. The inflection goes up at the end of an interrogative, and down at the end of a declarative sentence:

Is this grammar?
Boy, is it boring.

Punctuation, too, can have a radical effect on the meaning or perspective of a sentence. Consider the now famous example:

Woman without her man is nothing.

Woman: without her, man is nothing.

Not exactly the same sentiment.

Word Groups

English language functions are Naming, Predicating, Modifying and Connecting. A simple sentence comprises a subject and predicate whose functions are fulfilled by nouns and pronouns, verbs, adjectives and adverbs, and conjunctions and prepositions. **Nouns** are the subject of the sentence, and typically name or classify something or someone:

Studying <u>grammar</u> is boring.

Pronouns are substitutes for nouns. Their meaning can be found by referring to the original noun: He studied alone.

Some pronouns need no antecedent to make their meaning clear: Everyone dislikes studying grammar.

Verbs state or assert. They can indicate action: He <u>studied</u> his grammar lesson, an occurrence: He <u>was</u> home to study, or a state of being: He <u>appeared to be</u> studying.

The *infinitive* is the basic form of the verb, usually preceded by "to": He planned <u>to study</u> tonight.

Participles are verbs used as adjectives: <u>Hunched</u> over his book, he fell asleep.

Gerunds are the "ing" form of verbs used as nouns: His <u>studying</u> got him nowhere.

Modifiers, an extremely important and sometimes controversial word group, come in the form of *adjectives*, which modify nouns: Grammar is a <u>boring</u> subject, and *adverbs*, which modify verbs: He worked <u>diligently</u>, to no avail.

Prepositions, those words that can make a sentence excruciatingly passive, link nouns or pronouns to the rest of the sentence: I saw him <u>with</u> his grammar book.

Conjunctions join parts of the sentence: He failed the grammar test, <u>but</u> Stephanie passed.

Interjections, usually followed by a comma, are exclamatory words that express emotion: <u>Oh</u>, what a boring subject!

Elements of Consistency

Sentence structure is dependent on a number of other grammatical properties: tense, person, mood, number, voice, degree of formality, and point of view. These elements combine in harmony to make each sentence and paragraph flow smoothly into the next. A working knowledge of them is essential for clear, compelling, cohesive writing.

The six **tenses** relate to the time an action occurs.

Present: He rides the bus every day.

Past: He rode the bus every day.

Future: He will ride the bus every day from now on.

Present Perfect: He has ridden the bus every day so far.

Past Perfect: He had ridden the bus before.

Future Perfect: He will have ridden the bus every day by then.

Tense must remain consistent throughout the action and narration. The most common type of tense error no editor should ever have to correct is, "He walked to the door. He turns the knob and goes in."

Person refers to the form of pronoun and verb used to indicate the speaker or narrator. The three classifications are:

First

Singular: I go to the store.

Plural: We go to the store.

Novels written in the first person tell their tale or relate their information as if the writer were speaking of himself. This technique can be likened to a lecturer discussing a personal adventure, telling a story in which he is the central character, or imparting knowledge learned first-hand. Nonfiction written in the first person tends to follow an I/Thou structure: I have done this; you can, too.

Fiction written in the first person still uses second and third person as well, for dialogue and description, respectively.

Second

Singular: You go to the store.

Plural: You go to the store.

Nonfiction books written in the second person convey information or instructions geared to the specific reader: Once you have oiled the hinge, you can remove the door.

Second person is often the choice for self-help books. Novels are rarely written in the second person.

Third

Singular: He goes to the store.

Plural: They go to the store.

Most novels are written in third person. First-person fiction takes a special kind of skill, because the main character has to narrate all descriptions and must have a device for becoming aware of action or events at which he was not present.

Did You Know?

Donald Hamilton, who wrote the *Matt Helm* series of the 1960s, 70s and 80s in the first person, tells of receiving a call from a young author who wanted to talk about writing in the first person. Whether Hamilton was helpful is a matter of speculation; Tom Clancy's most successful books were written in the third person.

With the exception of I/Thou nonfiction, person should remain consistent throughout the book, regardless of changes in point of view. A heroine narrating a fiction in the first person, for example, should never refer to herself as "she," always as "I." A nonfiction writer chronicling the history of telephones in the third person should avoid personal statements such as "I think" or "I found."

Mood indicates how the speaker or narrator views the action. The three moods are:

Indicative: He is thirty years old.

Imperative: Tell me how old he is!

Subjunctive: I wish I looked as young as he does.

Moods fluctuate throughout a manuscript; however, fictional characters should remain true to their nature. An individual given to imperative dialogue would need a compelling reason to suddenly speak in a wistful, subjunctive mood.

Number refers to the singular and plural form of nouns, pronouns, verbs and so on:

He is walking the dog.

They are walking the dog.

Scholars who deplore the loss of formal English, however, often point with dismay to such everyday conversational usage as:

Each student should bring their grammar book to class

or:

They consider other people, surrounding them, with cast-offs of items that he doesn't use

("Gemini: May 21-June 21," distributed by Star City Distributors, Inc., Los Angeles, CA and Star City South, Atlanta, GA)

as evidence of modern illiteracy. Suffice to say, singular nouns require singular verb forms, plural nouns require plural verb forms.

Formal versus Informal

Exactly what **formality** refers to is a matter of some debate. In traditional terms, the level of formality was related primarily to using different noun and pronoun forms:

He is not as old as I am.

Whom shall I say is calling?

I do not know from whence he came.

In the modern sense, it also includes placing prepositions and using contractions:

He's not as old as me.

Who's calling?

I don't know where he came from.

As late as the mid 1990s, informal English was considered incorrect English, and the matter is still one of controversy between those who wish to retain the elegance of the language and those who prefer to make it more accessible. When trying to decide whether you want to write formally or informally, consider your audience's educational level, the subject's viability and the tone you want for your manuscript. Dialogue, for example, should sound like conversation. People seldom use "proper" English when speaking in today's world, but they might if your story is set in the eighteenth or nineteenth century.

Contractions are another academic vs. commercial topic. Traditionally, neither fiction nor nonfiction permitted the use of contractions: don't can't, isn't, would've, thanks, 'bye and so on. In today's marketplace, that attitude is arcane. Since the written word chronicles the author's times, confining yourself to old or academic speech patterns or language is anti-constructive unless you're writing to an academic audience or in a historical setting.

Contractions, like idioms, are also good devices for distinguishing characters native to English from those who came to the language later, as only English uses contractions in both speech and writing. Hence, a conversation between a New Yorker and a Frenchman, for example, might read:

"Hi, Pierre, how's it going?"

"Hello, Steve. I am doing well, thank you."

but probably not:

"Hello, Pierre, how are you?"

"Pretty good, Steve, thanks."

"Thanks" is a contraction, "pretty good" an idiom and both are only readily understood by Americans.

Spelling

It's almost absurd to have to point out that "their" is not the same as "there" or "they're"; "it's" does not mean "its"; "shone" and "shown" are not synonyms; and while you might measure something's "length" and "width," you cannot measure its "heighth." Furthermore, with all due respect to Ebonics, the past tense of "look" is "looked" with an "ed" suffix, but the past tense of "see" is "saw." Don't count on your word processor's spell checker—look it up.

Typographical Errors

Unless you have time to walk away from the manuscript for several weeks, have a cold reader find whatever typographical errors and other minor irregularities are left. No matter how hard you try or what technique you use, your brain will "see" what it knows should be there rather than the actual little black marks on the paper.

A special note about fiction proofing: find someone who understands and regularly reads fiction and will not try to impose nonfiction grammar on the prose. In nonfiction, for example, the line, "Of course, you do," would normally have a comma after the interjection "of course." In fictional dialogue, however, including or not including that comma completely changes the meaning of the spoken line.

"Of course you do," is read with the emphasis on "Of course."

"Of course, you do," is read with the emphasis on "you" or "do."

The two-word phrase "of course" gives the sentence a specific rhythm that emphasizes either the phrase itself or the last word.

This is rhythmic nuance, another artistic aspect that cannot be taught. A good piece of fiction can be seriously damaged by someone who insists on academic, composition-style, or style-guide editing. Find yourself a fiction lover to do your final copy edit/proofread, or at least someone who has a light touch. After all, by the time the manuscript gets to this stage, it should only still retain those errors you lack the knowledge to correct, or that your mind refuses to see due to over-familiarity.

Points to Ponder

In a dictate more appropriate to the classroom than commercial prose, some editors insist you remove all "as" sentences from your writing. True, "as" constructions can be weak. For example, "His face grew dark. He drew his sword," is more powerful than "His face grew dark as he drew his sword." The "as" connector dilutes the impact of both actions. When one action prompts another, however, "as" can be perfectly acceptable: His stomach lurched as the skull rolled to a stop at his feet.

Adjectives and adverbs are often overused with little profit. "She was utterly appalled" is redundant. Appalled is a strong enough term to stand on its own, so "She was appalled" is sufficient. In the same vein, "relaxing luxuriously" is simply a question of the author refusing to choose a word, "relaxing" or "luxuriating." That kind of redundancy was acceptable in Dicken's day, when the author was paid by the word, but is rather wordy today.

Both "Thrusting his arms outward, he advanced forward, crying to the heavens" and "He thrust arms outward, advanced and cried to the heavens" may be grammatically correct, but "ing" verb forms of the former make for a weaker construction than the positive action sequence of the latter—and it would be tough to advance in any direction but forward.

Capitalization errors, such as using Mom when the person is being talked about (correct: "my mom told me to tell you...") or mom when the person is being addressed (correct: "Mom, did you bring me anything?) cannot be corrected by a computer spell-check program. You either have to understand these kinds of subtleties or have an editor who does.

Fragments, those banes of high-school English class, can be very powerful when used for emphasis. To be effective, however, they have to be short and pithy:

A fragment can be an effective device. Sometimes.

If the fragment is not used for emphasis, or if it continues for more than a single phrase, it turns into either a jarring error or a run-on sentence:

So we can make rapturous love.

When I saw her with all that makeup and her hair done up just so and her dress skin tight like that.

Hyphenated and split words may give your computer's spell checker apoplexy. Taxi cab, taxi-cab or taxicab? When in doubt, don't rely on Microsoft's database; check out an Oxford, Random House, American Heritage or Webster's dictionary.

Sometimes, authors fall in love with the sound of a word or series of words, even if those words are misused: The sun's brilliant rays blinded me as it filtered through the windshield. If the rays are so brilliant as to be blinding, they cannot be filtering through the windshield; they must be either beaming or shining or radiating. Here's another one:

...like a lion languidly stalking his prey.

Similes are great, aren't they? But they have to make sense. Lions do not languidly stalk their prey or anything else.

If they're stalking, they're not languid; if they're languid, their prey has nothing to fear at the moment. An amateur might want to call it an oxymoron, but it's actually just incorrect word choice.

Apparently an entire generation of students was never introduced to the concept of multiple-word modifiers. If you have a **gray, shapeless hat**, use a comma between gray and shapeless to indicate that the hat is both gray and shapeless. If the modifiers were reversed, you could write **shapeless gray hat** without any commas to indicate that "shapeless" is actually modifying "gray hat." Then again, if the shapeless hat is dark gray, then the noun, hat, is being modified by both the shape (or lack thereof) and a two-word color, dark gray, which gets hyphenated into one term, dark-gray. Hence, you have a **shapeless, dark-gray hat**. Of course, some editors will leave it as a **shapeless dark-gray hat**—and only an English teacher or style-guide-oriented editor will care.

If'n it ain't no good, then it is good, and if'n your character doesn't know that, he'd better be ethnic, a good 'ole boy or blatantly uneducated.

According to the standardized rules, sentences may never begin with "And," "But," "Hopefully," "Although," "As" or "While." And while that concept is fine for graded compositions, it's outmoded for modern commercial work. Such structures, when used sparingly, provide the same kind of emphasis and sharp focus as a well-placed fragment.

Bottom line: the trick is to comprehend the rules of syntax and good writing well enough to know when to apply them and when to disregard them. A good editor will understand this concept. A generic editor who revises your work "by the book" may end up doing more harm than good.

Over Editing, Intrusive Editing

Many aspiring authors honestly believe their prose really only needs a "light edit," and are aghast when their manuscript comes back covered in red ink. Sometimes, though, they're right. After all, there is no force more powerful in the universe than the urge to alter someone else's words. Beware of over editing! Here is a prime example of a poem that required no change whatsoever (poetry is seldom open to editorial alteration by anyone other than the author), but was "corrected" simply due to the editor's internal urges.

HOW TO BE A JEWISH GRANDMOTHER

or

Throw In a Little Piece Parsley; Shouldn't be a Total Loss

So here you are, a JGM *new*
And, whaddya know, of twins! *bit of ?*
Here comes a (little) good advice
(With tongue in cheek and grins).

The key is that the parents, *yuk. We don't Talk this way —*
Barely out of childhood grown,
With your tactful domination
Must be guided, must be shown.

Bear in mind your viewpoint
Is the only one that counts
~~Give them~~ your vainglorious words *should echo*
In copious amounts.

The parents, of course, know nothing
Their experience is nil
But you, my dear, have done it all
With superincumbent skill.

Remember well the power of guilt
As handed down to you
Choose familiar ~~A couple of~~ platitudes ~~are nice~~
To casually *havent and To* strew.

And *theres when* ~~now that~~ everybody knows
Exactly who is boss
Throw in a little piece parsley--
Shouldn't be a total loss.

--by (2x) Great Aunt Ellen (1-03)

8
Submissions

The Nonfiction Proposal

Fact: nonfiction books are sold via proposal. The proposal is a marketing device, pure and simple. It entices a publisher to offer a contract and a check based solely on its projection of what the book will ultimately be and who will eventually want to buy it. It is not a rewrite of the book's contents, but a sales brochure that entices the reader to "come into the showroom and see for yourself."

Writing good proposals is practically an art in itself, and dozens of books are available on how to craft exactly what agents and publishers want to read. For true insider advice, see agent Jeff Herman's *Writer's Guide to Book Editor, Publishers and Literary Agents* or *Write the Perfect Book Proposal: 10 Proposals that Sold and Why,* agent Michael Larsen's *How to Write A Book Proposal,* agent Judith Applebaum's *How to Get Happily Published . . .* the list is almost endless.

Rather than attempt to reinvent the wheel, therefore, the following guidelines are offered merely to familiarize you with the elements of the proposal package.

From Finish to Start

The complete package opens with a Cover Page followed by a Contents page, the document itself, and two or three sample chapters. The finished document sections should read more or less in this order: the Overview, Competition, Marketing, Author Bio, Promotion, Book Details and Book Contents.

Do Not try to write a proposal in its final order
Write it in the Exact Opposite order

Some agents prefer the Author Bio after the Overview or the Marketing section before the Competition section. Marketing and Competition can also be subsections of the Overview, with Promotion a subsection of the Author Bio. These variations are not deal-breaking issues.

Begin by focusing, developing and structuring the entire book as if you were, indeed, going to write the whole manuscript. Put together the **Sample Chapters**. Then complete the **Book Contents**, **Book Details** and **Author Bio** and **Promotion** sections. Finally, do the **Competition** and **Marketing** sections or subsections. By the time you get to the **Overview**, you will be so totally immersed in the material that you will have no trouble expressing exactly what the book is and why the right publisher needs to buy it right now. Along those lines, therefore, the following information is provided in the order of the work, *not* in the order of the final document.

Book Contents

Flesh out the project map you created when you structured the material into explicit chapter-by-chapter descriptions (see chapter 5). Limit the one-paragraph blurbs to approximately 100 words each, and add any additional points in a short bulleted list, if necessary. If you are dealing with a true crime, memoir or other material that lends itself to a story format, you can substitute a synopsis. Avoid using outlines, which tend to make sense to the author but not to a cold reader.

Chapter 1. The author convenes his first group therapy session for sons and daughters of celebrities. He goes on to spend almost two decades helping celebrity children and young adults deal with the issues inherent in hav-

Book Details

Multiply the average number of words in the sample chapters by the number of projected chapters to determine the approximate word count of the final draft. This one- or two-paragraph section also contains the estimated number of illustrations, maps, charts, photographs, drawings and so on; the number of appendices, if any, and whether or not the book will require an index. Include information on any special features, such as an accompanying workbook, as well as the time needed to complete the manuscript.

Most large publishers buy for two years in the future so they look for a 10-12 month lead-time unless the manuscript is already completed. Be aware that an overly long lead-time or excessive amount of special—read "expensive"—features can kill a book deal. Common errors include not including this section, not providing a relatively accurate count of non-text material, or not mentioning that the book is finished and has been edited by an independent professional, a money-*saving* feature.

Short and concise, *What Happened Then* will run approximately 36,750 words and include five to seven charts and diagrams, all of which will be embedded into the manuscript. Two appendices will comprise an additional 7,000 words: "Practical Advice" and " Getting the Most Out of Your Program." The manuscript can be completed within a ten-to-twelve month period.

Author Bio

A one-page section, this is merely the author's bio emphasizing those credentials that lend authority to her writing the book. If you are not the bylined author, **do not mention your contribution**. If you are the bylined author, do not include falsehoods or any hint of overstatement or exaggeration of your expertise. Make sure you provide sufficient proof of your knowledge and/or authority on the subject.

> Jane Doe is an expert in the transformation of women and relationships, having worked with more than a thousand women before and since acquiring her Ph.D. in Women's Studies and Transpersonal Psychology from America University in Anytown, OH in 1968.
>
> As Chair of the Master of Arts Degree in Women and the Transpersonal Perspective at America University, she has been teaching all aspects of feminine consciousness, spirituality and relationality for the past several years, including such feminine/spiritual combination classes as "The Heroine's Journey," "Women's Ways of Knowing," and "Spiritual Emergence." Her articles on the feminine and relationships have appeared in *Dimensions Magazine*, an east-coast regional publication.
>
> Jane Doe has honed her ability to inspire and mentor women during the 15-year course of her private practice, and while serving as the director of a single-parent-and-homemaker program called Make Love Not Angst. Not only has she helped hundreds of women relationally mentor their husbands, she credits the process for the longevity of her own marriage. Jane Doe currently lives in Someplace, West Virginia, with her husband of thirty-three years.

Promotion

Either as part of the above or sub-sectioned, note your speaking, entertainment or other public-forum experience and/or attributes that will make you a desirable talk-show, seminar, conference, etc., guest or speaker, and list how you personally plan to promote the book to the public. The most common errors in this section are not including it, being vague about your plans, or appearing less than enthusiastic about promoting your own book.

> John Smith plans to participate in a two-front promotional campaign for *Safe, Effective Confronting*. Professional seminars will teach therapists how to teach confronting while laymen seminars will help individuals understand the need for this step-by-step process. John will also make himself available for an author's tour including TV, radio and print interviews and book signings, and include all promo-

tional and scheduling information on his website, John Smith's Web. The two promotional campaigns will run concurrently; John plans to hire a professional publicist to help coordinate scheduling.

Marketing

In two to four paragraphs, describe who will want to read the book, the size of that market, and how to reach those readers. A biography of Abraham Lincoln, for example, would not only appeal to people who enjoy biographies, but to historians, students, Civil-War enthusiasts, etc. Possible markets would be both online and brick-and-mortar book-stores, museums, historical societies, history and biography book clubs, re-enactment festivals, academic buyers and so forth. Common errors in this section are vagueness and defining an overly narrow or broad audience.

Every individual in America who deals with children – every parent, teacher, school administrator, doctor, social worker, counselor, attorney, judge and advocate – needs to read *Mothers Against Sexual Abuse* (MASA). While that goal may not be attainable, every parent whose child is being molested or raped will be grateful for the information in these pages--information that until now could only be found scattered in various pamphlets or scholarly treatises.

Due to the epidemic of child sexual abuse (CSA) in this country, *Mothers Against Sexual Abuse* can be placed naturally in all trade and mass-market stores, in addition to being distributed throughout the expanding MASA network. Women's centers, child-abuse retreats, rape-crises clinics, and other protection agency outlets will find *Mothers Against Sexual Abuse* an invaluable, long-overdue reference and "how-to" guide.

Competition

Reference a minimum of three to a maximum of five current and/or standard-of-the-industry titles that cover the same or similar material as your book, and illustrate how this book refocuses, corrects, expands or in any other way adds to the field of knowledge on the topic. Expend no more than one brief paragraph per book. The purpose is to demonstrate your awareness of the field and to give the reader an idea of where this contribution fits into the knowledge base already available without belittling a competing author or denigrating the theories behind a published title. Common competition errors include references that are too old, ignoring important or bestselling titles, insufficient comparisons and overkill or suspect analysis.

Despite the unqualified acceptance of confronting as an indispensable tool in many healing programs, literary support material is virtually unavailable. *Healing the Shame That Binds You* by John Bradshaw (HCI 1988), for example, discusses the confront process in a mere page, just long enough to emphasize the simplistic approach of expressing feelings without assigning guilt, yet remaining assertive throughout. Although well-intentioned, Mr. Bradshaw does not discuss how to prepare, set up, or evaluate the confront. Other typical "How-To" books, such as *It's Not What You're Eating, It's What's Eating You,* (Janet Greensen, Ph.D., Pocket Books 1990), concentrate on the "When You...I Felt...I Need..." aspect of expressing past pain. While certainly stating the need and potential benefits of confronting, these volumes provide no constructive information on how to avoid having this "feelings" episode blow up in the reader's face. Still others, like *The Sexual Healing Journey: A Guide for Survivors of Sexual Abuse* by Wendy Maltz (Harper 1991), avoid the subject altogether, stating only that the reader may have to confront a former or currently abusive person at some point.

With literally dozens of books on the market advocating confrontation, *Safe, Effective Confronting* is more than a welcome addition to the burgeoning field of self-help, recovery and self-healing—it is an absolute necessity.

The Overview

The longest section of the report, this two-and-a-half to four-page summary should *describe* the book's content, not explore it. As a marketing piece meant to entice someone into signing a check with your name on it, the Overview must be comprehensive and compelling, hooking the reader in the same first paragraph that states the who, what, why, when, and how of the book while keeping in mind the four "U"s of advertising: Unique, Urgent, Useful and Ultra-Specific.

*I love him, but I've outgrown him. The bottom line is that I've
changed and he hasn't. I know I can go on without him, but I really don't want a
divorce—I want him to grow with me. Is that wrong?*

Women have indeed changed. In the last thirty years, a
nanosecond in history, women have not only altered the social and
political landscape of our country, they've changed themselves. The
one area that hasn't changed, however, is intimacy. Relationships.
Marriage. Man courting woman. Man as cave-dwelling brooder,
woman as nurturing helpmate. *The Feminine Shift: Changing the World
One Man at a Time* is the first book to define man/woman intimacy
from a feminine perspective, and state what millions of women across
America intuitively know: women have inherently superior relational
skills and aptitudes. They don't need to change, men do. Not for the
woman's sake, but for the man's, and for the future of their lives together. And since the male animal admittedly cannot change by himself, his female mate needs to mentor him.

Subsequent paragraphs should explain the scope of the
material, the need for the book and your expertise and reason
for writing it. **Do not reproduce the book's text in the
Overview**. Use active verbs whenever possible, such as "ex-
plores," "explains," "demystifies," "demonstrates," "uncov-
ers" and so on, but do not be overly concerned about passive
voice. This is one piece of writing where "tell" wins over
"show."

Common **Overview** errors include overwriting (too long)
or being sketchy (too short); not having a hook; using a dog-
matic, pleading, bitter, journalistic or academic tone; showing
or demonstrating rather than telling; using emotion-laden
rather than emotionally charged prose and simply not making
a convincing case for the book. Like any good promotion, the
material has to be exciting but informative, entertaining but
factual.

Title Page and Contents

Use the same format for the proposal's title page as you
would for a manuscript. Use conventional manuscript for-

matting for the Contents page, listing the proposal's, not the book's, contents with page numbers.

Points to Remember

Be sure you include the **first two or three chapters** of the book, polished as if they were ready for publication. If the opening chapters are not compelling, get rid of them. Keep in mind, however, that since books are often restructured as they are written, these sample chapters will probably not appear "as is" when you finish the rest of the book.

Edit, edit and re-edit. Keep the formatting simple and double-check to make sure all the headers, headings and page numbers are consistent and clear. Double-space all copy. Have the final draft proofread by a cold eye and leave the pages loose; do not bind or staple. Remember, a proposal is advertising; make it sparkle.

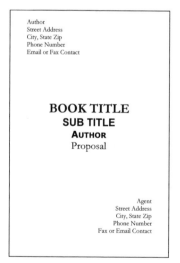

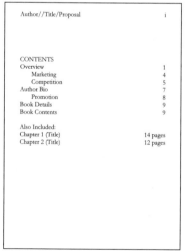

Synopsis

Simply put, the synopsis tells the story of your novel. If the synopsis is not sound, the chapters may not even be read; therefore, it must be articulate, captivating and devoid of digressions and details. Keep background information to a minimum, descriptions of main characters brief. Secondary characters need not be mentioned by name, minor characters need not be mentioned at all. The most radical differences between a manuscript and synopsis, though, is in the presentation of the story: while you *unfold* the story in a manuscript, usually in the past tense, you *tell* it in a synopsis in the present tense.

Do not try to sell the book with the same synopsis you used to put it together. The former will probably have changed in the course of writing, and may contain details noted for your emphasis only. The latter must conform exactly to the finished story line and include a minimum of distracting details, descriptions, character analysis and so on. Do not omit the ending; this is not a back-of-the-book teaser, it is a marketing tool.

The easiest way to create a synopsis is to go through your manuscript and write a one-two sentence summary of what happens in each chapter. Eventually you will have the entire course of the story in sequential order. Refine and polish the summary, deleting any extraneous information that does not directly add to the flow of the story from start to finish. Avoid all unnecessary modifiers and understood action; e.g., "Mary finds Ralph making love to her sister, rushes home, and returns with her gun," rather than "Mary went up to Ralph's apartment, found him making love to her sister. Shocked and dismayed, she rushed home, tore her house apart until she found her gun, then returned to Ralph's apartment."

How long should a synopsis be? Good question! Authorities agree it should absolutely be a few paragraphs, two to three pages, eight to 10 pages, no less than 15-20 pages....

To make sure you have exactly whatever the agent or publisher wants, do three versions: brief, or one page; short, or three to five pages; and full, or 10-20 pages. That way, you will be prepared with whatever you need when someone says, "Yes, send it." Regardless of length, the project will sell or be defeated on the strength of the writing and the story, so once again—hone your skills.

Queries

The two opposing schools of thought about how query letters should be written are essentially held by the two different types of acquisition editors and agents who read them. The most prominent school of thought, supported by many fiction editors, some nonfiction editors and most agents, holds that a query letter should begin with an ad-copy-type opening, a statement so dramatic, funny or startling as to immediately capture the attention, thereby (theoretically) prompting a "hunger" to obtain and read at least a synopsis or proposal, if not the entire manuscript.

Since the sole purpose of a query letter is not to secure a contract but merely to elicit an invitation to submit, this method certainly has the advantage of whetting the reader's appetite.

> Terrified neighbors woke to a woman screaming for help and a man's voice crying, "If I can't have you, nobody can!" Shots rang out. Police attribute Mary Jane Segal's death to a former lover she hadn't dated in almost a year — yet another case of "fatal attraction."

The second type of editor, however, would rather not be "hyped," preferring instead to have his or her interest raised by the subject stated plainly and briefly. A great many nonfiction editors prefer this approach, as it lends itself to a shorter letter that gets to the point immediately and subsequently, to a quicker review and easier decision-making process.

> In 1979, approximately 12,500[*] people were killed by lovers suffering from "fatal attractions"; just one decade later, that figure topped 37,000. I propose to do a survey book exploring this alarming trend...

The type of book, as well as the person to whom you are sending it, will usually dictate which approach to use. A non-fiction treatment of the military options in Iraq being offered directly to an appropriate acquisitions editor, for example, would be best presented using the plainer, more concise query style. A fiction wrapped around the same basic subject and submitted to an agent might be more effectively promoted using the dramatic approach.

Using the wrong approach can result in a rejection that narrows the field of solicitation, despite how (theoretically) appropriate the material is for the publisher. Feedback is seldom provided to explain if the problem lies in the idea, the author's credentials, the current market, or the letter itself. Therefore, the query itself, like the proposal package, must be as finely tuned as possible to prevent it from being an inadvertent obstacle to serious consideration.

Format

A query letter not only sells the idea behind the book, it also presents a convincing case as to why you should be the one to write it. Since it is your first contact with the individual from whom you want an invitation to submit your manuscript, make sure it is as clean and polished as that manuscript. The query demonstrates your professionalism, attention to detail and writing ability.

Propose only one idea per letter. If you try to contract for a series of books, you may exhaust your contacts without ever

---

[*] Not real figures

receiving an invitation to submit even one proposal, much less a manuscript. Avoid overly friendly or stuffy language, gimmicks and manipulative devices. Never make demands or threats, or insinuate that the reader "will be sorry" to pass up your great piece of work. Keep your query focused and straightforward. Single space using conventional business-letter margins, and—unless you are including a *short* fictional synopsis as part of the letter—accomplish your purpose within the space of a single page.

You can use the same query whether writing to literary agents or acquisition editors, but make sure you personalize the letter with the specific name, title and address of the person you are trying to reach. Never send to "XYZ Literary Agency" or "Editor in Chief." Sending letters or materials to people who do not deal with your subject or genre is simply a waste of everyone's time and your postage. And keep in mind that while American life has gotten quite informal overall, business etiquette dictates a more formal approach when writing to someone you do not know. You will make a better impression with "Dear Mr. Litage" than with "Dear Bob" or the email-friendly, "Hi, Bob!"

Research

While *Literary Market Place (LMP)* is the acknowledged "bible" of the book industry, it is **not** a good research tool when looking for agents or publishers as it gives no specific information. Many people swear by Writer's Digest's *Writer's Market*, but the best reference book on the market is actually Jeff Herman's *Writer's Guide to Book Editors, Publishers and Literary Agents*. A literary agent himself, Jeff updates *Writer's Guide* at least once a year with specific information on what each individual is looking for, does not want to see, and how best to make contact, thus making it easier to determine which agents and/or publishers might be interested in your particular manuscript.

On the Internet, check for agents at the "Association of Author Representatives" (AAR), "Guide to Literary Agents" and "Agents Actively Looking." (Please see Appendix for all URLs). Thousands of individual agents also have web sites of their own. Look for someone who is an AAR member, which means he or she does not charge a reading fee and is actually in the business of selling books to publishers, not exacting fees from authors for rewrites or edits.

To check for publishers, go to "Bowker's Publishers HomePages" or "Publishers Marketing Association."

Expect to send out five to 12 queries each month until you get an offer from an agent or publisher. If you are consistently rejected without being asked for the proposal or manuscript, the problem is probably your letter, not your ideas. Rewrite and try again.

Unless otherwise noted in one of the above references, send your proposal or manuscript only to those who request it and print "**Requested Material**" on the outside of the envelope or box. Again, never bind or staple the manuscript, synopsis or proposal.

Query Follow up

You can get one of three possible reactions from your query letter: 1) a positive response, requesting the proposal or synopsis, sample chapters or full manuscript, 2) a negative response, turning down the idea or 3) no response, which can mean anything from the letter or reply having been lost in the mail, to the lack of a self-addressed, stamped reply envelope or postcard, to the individual not having gotten to it yet

In the first two cases, your own response is clear cut: a positive reply calls for submission of the requested material; a negative reply calls for you to continue your search efforts in another direction. The third reaction—no response—is the one that so often frustrates and confounds the writer. How long are you supposed to wait? Should you follow up a query with another letter, or perhaps a phone call? What if the second contact fares no better? Doesn't a lack of response really mean "no?"

In theory, most editors and agents profess to answer all query letters within two to four weeks; in practice, that time frame is seldom easy to achieve. Acquisition editors and literary agents get a continuous, heavy flow of mail. Simply sorting and reading through it all is a tremendously time-consuming job—and not their sole, much less primary, function. Three or four weeks is not an unreasonable length of time to wait for your query to get read, approved or disapproved and returned to you. By the same token, wondering what has become of your letter is hardly unreasonable, either. While some agents and/or editors may, indeed, use a lack of response to indicate "no," most will accord you the courtesy of a specific answer when they have had the chance to read your letter and consider your project.

Following up a query letter after approximately six weeks is quite reasonable. You can send a brief note, make a quick phone call or e-mail a short reminder, if you have the appropriate address. Follow-up letters sent through the mails or by fax can be followed up, in turn, with a phone call if no response is given within another four to six weeks. When writing, you may want to send a copy of the original query, in the event the first was lost in the mail or the corporate system. The note should be short and concise, indicating the number of weeks that have passed since the initial contact, and requesting an indication as to interest in the project. Maintain a professional, non-belligerent tone throughout, of course.

Check with the individual's secretary to determine the best time to call. Keep phone calls short, professional and friendly. Angry or teary demands as to why a letter has not been answered will only result in a negative impression, thereby defeating your purpose.

Once you have secured a positive response, the submission is considered **solicited**. Send *exactly* what the agent or editor requests, regardless of advice from other writers or books. The traditional route has been to secure publishing interest through a well-honed proposal before writing a non-fiction book—today, however, some acquisition editors want to see more of the actual manuscript. Fiction is another matter: finish and polish your first novel before you begin sending out queries to submit it. When an editor or agent wants support material rather than the manuscript, they are referring to a proposal for nonfiction and a full synopsis for fiction.

Whether they admit it or not, most agents and editors have a 30-second rule—if you do not catch their interest in the first 30 seconds, you've lost them entirely. If you do catch their interest, they'll read for about three minutes. If you haven't kept their attention the material goes into a reject pile; if you have, it gets put aside for a more thorough reading later. With this prevalent secret in mind, keep your cover letter short and interesting so the page gets turned and the reader gets to the heart of your material—be it proposal, synopsis, or sample chapters—within that first 30 seconds. Ideally, once anyone gets into the meat of the matter they won't be able to put it down.

Submission Follow up

Once you have submitted a package or manuscript, you're back to waiting. This period, hopefully, will be longer rather than shorter, for the editor or agent now has a difficult decision to make. Proposals and sample chapters take quite a bit longer to read and absorb than letters, manuscripts even longer. In fact, a quick response is most often a negative reply—editors interested in a project will route it to a supervisor, an editorial committee or the marketing department before contacting you. Follow up if the response time the agent or editor originally estimated has elapsed. As with the query, the communication should be brief, polite and focused.

Don't just wait, work. Finish the manuscript. Start a second book. Do not sit by the phone or mailbox; that only makes time seem to go slower. **Keep a log** of exactly when and to whom you sent out each letter and submission so you do not fall into the trap of thinking, "It's been months!" when, in fact, your letter only went out three weeks ago.

When you send out five query letters, receive three positive responses and a subsequent publishing offer, the world is beautiful and life is wonderful—and you should be playing the lottery. The road is not normally so smooth for most writers, especially first-time authors. Five query letters sent within the proper market can easily result in five negative responses; three submissions can become three turndowns within a single week. At some point, you are going to start reflecting on what is being rejected, the idea, the presentation or the writing. The question is, when does that point occur?

Accepting a mere three or four rebuffs as the basis for a rewrite is self-defeating, unless the same problem has been noted in two or more personal notes. When the number of turn-downs starts to reach toward the teens, though, you might want to re-examine where the process is bogging down. If a widely submitted query letter has not produced an invitation to submit, the fault could lie in either the idea or the letter. Perhaps you did not demonstrate sufficient background for the subject at hand; maybe the idea itself has been overworked in the market. If the idea and your credentials are sound, the competition not excessive and the market well-targeted, the problem probably lies in the presentation: the query letter itself. Is it too friendly or formal? Overly detailed or superficial? Whatever the specific problem, scrap the thing and rewrite.

Some books only appeal to very specialized audiences, and an author can exhaust the entire potential market by using an ineffective query letter. Publishers and agents who have rejected an idea at the query stage are seldom enticed into extending an invitation through a second missive. Be as sensitive as you can to the cause of rejection. If the problem is indeed the concept, keep searching until you find the correct publisher/market. On the other hand, when you get rejected because you have no apparent basis to write the book, or because your initial contact was ineffectual, you have to consider the door definitively closed.

Did You Know?

Even Jimmy Carter, formerly the most powerful man in the world and author of some half-dozen published titles, has to provide a book proposal for every new book he wants to pitch.

Proposal Rejection

A submission package must shine. Consistent rejection at this level indicates 1) the market or competition was not researched thoroughly enough, 2) the idea or story was not sufficiently developed, 3) the writing was simply not up to par or 4) you are not submitting to the appropriate publishers for your "niche."

Re-evaluate not only your idea or plot but your ability, credentials, and background as well. Possibly all you need is an outside edit. On the other hand, you may need to take an entirely fresh approach. A writers' critique group might be of some help. Oftentimes, a package that is "close" is rejected with a personal note explaining the obstacle for the agent or editor, which leaves you a clear path for correcting or restructuring the proposal to resubmit. If, however, the package is being rejected out-of-hand via one form letter after another, the writing is probably just not worthy of professional consideration. You might want to consider taking some classes to get the personal perspective of a knowledgeable instructor, or having a professional critique to help you get back on track.

When all is said and done, though, you must remember this is a type of game in which the players change often. A proposal rejected from one agent or acquisition editor might be picked up by another agent or even an editor in a different department—or the new guy who replaced your rejecter two weeks later. Take the case of *Cop To Call Girl*, which got turned down **200 times** before being picked up by—you guessed it—the very first publisher the author had ever contacted! People change jobs, book-list needs ebb and flow, the economy goes up and down, assistant readers have fights with their spouses...all these aspects really do affect whether or not your manuscript gets picked up by any given agent or editor on any given day. Don't get discouraged, and don't rewrite something you believe in until you've had at least one *qualified* professional tell you what is wrong. Think what those 22 acquisition editors who turned down *Harry Potter* must feel like today....

About Literary Agents

Literary agents offer a number of significant advantages to both aspiring authors and author/writers. They have current knowledge of not only the industry as a whole, but the general trends within the business and the windows of opportunity available in the major publishing houses and imprints. They often have personal contacts in those publishing houses and usually are known, at least on a name-recognition basis, by the people to whom they are pitching.

Of course, there are also disadvantages to working or attempting to work with a literary agent. It can take longer to get picked up by an agent than to secure a publishing contract. You lose control over, and up-to-the-minute knowledge of which publishers are reading your manuscript and when and why they reject it. Once you've signed with an agent, he will seldom call unless he has an offer to convey or you owe him money. All of the above makes sense when you understand the average literary agent's function and workload. Agents do not earn any income from reading manuscripts, writing rejection notes or giving away free advice on the phone, in personal notes or via email. Nevertheless, these occupations can take up a significant portion of their day.

One well-known agency kept track in 1997 and found that at the end of the year, it had received 3,064 query letters. That's over 255 letters every month, almost 60 letters per week. That's a lot of mail over and above actual business. Yet, in a clear indication of this business' reality, the agents only asked to see about a dozen of those manuscripts, *less than one-half percent.*

What makes an agent reject a project at the query stage? First and foremost, a poorly written letter that demonstrates the writer's lack of book-industry knowledge, attention to detail, writing talent or all of the above. Secondly, most agents are constantly queried about projects they would never handle, even though a quick check either in *Writer's Guide* or on their web site will furnish a clear picture of where their interests lie. Furthermore, since your query provides a first-impression glimpse of you as a writer, why would someone who devotes her life to a literary pursuit give serious consideration to a letter full of grammatical or punctuation errors, misspellings or awkward sentences?

The sheer volume of queries agents have to field precludes their asking for more than a few manuscripts at any given time. Of those that they read, they can only afford to put their time, money and efforts behind the ones they really like, and really believe they have the knowledge, contacts and ability to sell. Most agents will tell you they take on less than 3% of everything submitted to them. And, since only a relative handful of the tens of thousands of publishers in this country will 1) work through an agent and 2) provide enough of an advance to adequately compensate for an agent's time and pains, they have a finite number of places to which they can submit your manuscript, after they've done all the leg-work necessary to ferret out at least initial interest via phone calls or their own query letters. Despite their best efforts, **few literary agents sell more than a small percentage of the projects they take on, yet they only make money on those projects that sell.**

In light of all this, you may find it more understandable that literary agents only call when:

- They have an offer for you
- They get a request to change something in the manuscript
- They receive a contract for you
- You make the *New York Times, LA Times* or *Boston Globe* bestseller list
- You're going to be on Oprah, Good Morning America or the six o'clock evening news
- You owe them money

The Top of the Pile

If you want to be one of the select few picked up by any given agent, you must be prepared to compete with the top one percent of those 6,000,000 circulating manuscripts. To achieve that goal, you must know your market niche and where you fit in. Your query must be succinct and professional, with the finished nonfiction proposal or full novel flawless and ready to send. You must accept the delay inherent in the submission process and recognize the value of working, rather than waiting; dropping a postcard or note rather than calling; and moving on to another potential agent rather than pestering one who has already said "no."

Simply put, learn your craft, learn your business, be a pro.

Agent Personas

Contrary to any bad press you may have read, the overwhelming majority of bona fide agents put forth 100% of their effort for their clients. That effort lands them roughly into one of four general categories:

- The **Sprinter**, who begins your relationship with a flurry of activity and communication, but moves on if your manuscript does not sell within the first four or five months.

- The **Fade Out**, who covers all the bases and tries his best, but never actually lets you know when he has done all he can for you.

- The **Long Haul**, who will hang onto your manuscript for five years, if necessary, and send it out whenever she sees the window of opportunity re-open—but does not want to talk to you in the meantime.

- The **Ideal,** who sells your book in less than six weeks for a seven-figure advance in a four-book deal plus movie rights and nominates you for the Nobel Prize in Literature in his spare time.

As you might suspect, that last character is a work of fiction.

Did You Know?

No member of the Association of Authors' Representatives (AAR) is permitted to charge any kind of fee, including reading fees, monthly or yearly retainers or "management" fees. However, the agent/author contract can stipulate reimbursement for photocopies, USPS postage or any mail or messenger service delivery charges.

9
Publishing

To publish literally means "to prepare and issue (printed material) for public distribution or sale" (*The American Heritage Dictionary, Fourth Edition,* Houghton Mifflin Company, 2001). In other words, publishing is the act of creating a finished product from a manuscript and generating copies of that product for public sale. In accordance with that definition, 21st century publishing comprises **Acquisition**, **Prepress** and **Production** but *not* Distribution, Promotion, Marketing or Selling the product. Those functions, while necessary to recoup the expense of publishing, are handled by separate departments or entities and consequently require separate operations.

Perhaps the most confusing aspect of 21st century publishing is the array of new technological buzz words that makes it appear publishing has radically changed when, in fact, these terms primarily refer to either new formats or production techniques.

Digital publishing is a production term that means the book can be transferred directly from computer files to a high-speed laser printer. Those files can be developed in any number of word-processing, page-layout and publishing programs that allow you to create the entire work onscreen before converting into Adobe PDF (Portable Document Format) or Microsoft LIT (Literature). Pictures and drawings that previously required lengthy, expensive separation and printing processes can now be rasterized into bitmap-based formats, such as JPEG, GIF, TIFF, PNG, PICT and BMP, for immediate digital printing, or simply saved to a CD or uploaded to the Internet for ebook viewing. In fact, the simplicity and low cost of digitization has not only made it easier for smaller houses to publish more books at a higher profit, it has led to an explosion of production houses that can offer competitive prices for short-run book printings of 500 copies or less.

Adobe PDF and **Microsoft LIT** are the two most popular **portable file formats.** Unlike a standard word-processing file, a portable file can be viewed on any computer in the exact layout and design as it appears on the original computer. MS Word files, for example, sent over the Internet via attachment to an email message may appear on the receiver's screen with different margins or fonts than the originator's. Once the file is converted to a PDF or LIT format, the document appears exactly the same way, regardless of the receiver's computer settings, provided the receiver has the program to view that format. PDF is currently the standard for sending files across the Internet and for many ebooks. LIT is primarily an ebook format, used by a variety of Microsoft handheld ebook readers.

Rasterize means to convert vector graphic files into printable bitmap graphic files. A **vector graphic** is a two-dimensional picture or drawing saved and displayed in vectors rather than points. This makes it scaleable; that is, it can be made larger or smaller without losing its integrity. To be printable, vector graphics must be rasterized into **printable bitmap graphic** files, which are saved and displayed in points.

POD stands for Print On Demand, yet another name for the modern spin on a decades' old technique of printing the pages of a book straight off the computer just as you would a manuscript. Also known as digital printing, POD employs high-speed digital laser printers that can churn out thousands of pages in the amount of time an office desk-jet would produce dozens. POD is useful for small runs under 1,000 or 2,500 copies, the smallest runs economical for conventional book manufacturing. The POD cost per book is significantly higher than the manufactured cost, but five-hundred books at $5.00 per book is still only $2,500, whereas twenty-five hundred books at $2.50 per book is $6,250—and you have to be able to get rid of 2,500 books. POD is used by traditional publishers, self-publishers, subsidy/vanity publishers and independent authors who want to test the marketing waters and pick up endorsements and publicity blurbs while circulating their submission materials.

Did You Know?

Acme Bookbinding of Boston produces small-run POD versions of out-of-print classics for Harvard University Press, which then takes orders for additional sales spurred by the books being visibly available. Thus, good books get a second chance without the excessive cost inherent in traditional offset printing.

---

ePublishers produce **ebooks**, which are formatted into Microsoft Reader (LIT) or Adobe Acrobat eBook Reader (PDF) files that can be downloaded from a web site onto a desktop computer, hand-held ebook reader or tablet PC. Ebooks can be secured by the ePublisher to prevent changing, notating, copying or even printing. New programs and formats are appearing on a regular basis to match expanding eReader technology.

Virtual Publishing is the one truly new publishing avenue, which actually exists outside the industry proper. Authors post their original or derivative fiction on personal, fanfic or paid sites, thereby gaining both immediate gratification from reader comments and the potential of being seen and picked up by a literary agent or traditional publisher.

Fanfic is shorthand for fan fiction. Fanfic authors rewrite or pick up where episodes of favorite TV shows or movies left off, or create new stories using those familiar characters.

On the plus side, authors who might never be known by anyone outside their own family/friend circle can get exposure, critique and sometimes valuable help from impartial readers. On the down side, writers still learning their craft who are uncertain of their abilities are easy prey for the equally inexperienced or unschooled, and may feel pressured to skew their technique, their perspective or even their characters and plots to satisfy a few readers who exploit the comparative anonymity of the Internet to demand more chapters, the next story or character/plot changes in accordance with their own agendas. In the early days of the Internet, a handful of authors made the news by having their talent spotted on various websites. By the beginning of the 21st Century, the web had become glutted with writer sites, making that avenue of submission a long shot, although not entirely fruitless.

Traditional Publishing

Traditional publishers make their money selling the books they publish. Despite all the other options available in today's marketplace, traditional publishing still carries the most prestige, offers the widest chance for success to the most authors and produces the largest number of successful, bestselling titles. Traditional publishing affords public recognition, status within the literary community, immediate financial reward without personal risk or production demands, the opportunity for critical review leading to further recognition and prestige and unquestioned literary credentials. Traditional publishers provide all aspects of prepress and production; distribute through established wholesaler, distributor and direct-sale connections; provide for all fulfillment services; and maintain all records and contract legalities including advances and royalty payments.

Acquisition

Traditional publishing is the only strata in which literary agents are still necessary, particularly if you want to submit to any of the imprints or divisions of the nation's five largest houses, generally referred to as the "Big Boys" of the business. The divisions and imprints listed alphabetically below were last updated January, 2004. By the time this book reaches your hands, they may have changed again.

HARPERCOLLINS PUBLISHERS

Access Press
Amistad Press
Avon
Caedmon
Ecco
Eos
Fourth Estate
HarperCollins
Harper Audio
HarperBusiness
HarperEntertainment
HarperLargePrint
HarperResource
Harper Design International
HarperSan Francisco
HarperTorch
Perennial
PerfectBound
Quill
Rayo
ReganBooks
William Morrow
William Morrow Cookbooks

HARPERCOLLINS CHILDREN'S BOOKS

Avon
EOS
Greenwillow Books
HarperFestival
HarperTempest
Joanna Cotler Books
HarperCollins Children's Books
Katherine Tegen Books
Laura Geringer Books
Trophy

HOUGHTON MIFFLIN COMPANY

Calabash
Classwell
College Division
Great Source
International Division
Riverside Publishing Company
School Division
Sunburst Technology

McDougal Littell   Trade and Reference Division
Promissor

PENGUIN GROUP (USA) (2nd Largest English-Language Publisher in the world, formerly U.S. Penguin Putnam)

ADULTS

Ace Books	Jove
Avery	New American Library
Berkley Books	Penguin
Dutton	Perigee
G.P. Putnam's Sons	Plume
Gotham	Riverhead Books
HPBooks	Viking
Jeremy P. Tarcher	

CHILDREN'S

Dial Books for Young Readers

Dutton Children's Books	Philornel
Firebird	Price Stern Sloan
Frederick Warne	Puffin Books
G.P. Putnam's Sons	Viking Children's Books
Grosset & Dunlap	

RANDOM HOUSE (Largest English-Language Publisher in the world)

BALLANTINE PUBLISHING GROUP

Ballantine Reader's Circle	Del Rey/Lucas Books
Ballantine Books	One World
Del Rey	

BANTAM DELL PUBLISHING GROUP

Bantam Hardcover	Domain
Bantam Mass Media	DTP
Bantam Trade Paperback	Fanfare
Crimeline	Island

Delacorte Press

Dell

Delta

Spectra

The Dial Press

CROWN PUBLISHING GROUP

Bell Tower

Crown Business

Crown Publishers, Inc.

Clarkson Potter

Harmony Books

Prima

Shaye Areheart Books

Three Rivers Press

DOUBLEDAY BROADWAY BOOKS

Broadway Books

Currency

Doubleday Books

Doubleday Religious
Publishing

Doubleday Image

Harlem Moon/Black Ink

Main Street Books

Nan A. Talese

KNOPF

Alfred A. Knopf

Anchor

Everyman's Library

Pantheon Books

Schocken Books

Vintage

RANDOM HOUSE TRADE PUBLISHING GROUP

Modern Library

Random House

RH Reading

R. H. Trade Paperback

Strivers Row

Villard Books

RANDOM HOUSE AUDIO

RH Audible

RH Audio

RH Audio Assets

RH Audio Dimensions

RH Audio Price-less

RH Audio Roads

RH Audio voices

RANDOM HOUSE CHILDREN'S BOOKS

Junie B. Jones

Magic Tree House

Seussville

KNOPF/DELACORTE/DELL YOUNG READERS GROUP

Alfred A. Knopf	Dell Dragonfly
Bantam	Dell Laurel-Leaf
Crown	Dell Yearling Books
David Fickling Books	Doubleday
Delacorte Press	Wendy Lamb Books

RH YOUNG READERS GROUP

Akiko	Mercer Mayer
Arthur	Nickelodeon
Barbie	Nick, Jr.
Beginner Books	pat the bunny
The Berenstain Bears	Picturebacks
Bob The Builder	Precious Moments
Disney	Sesame Street Books
First Time Books	Step into Reading
Golden Books	Stepping Stone
Landmark Books	Star Wars
Little Golden Books	Thomas the Tank Engine and
Lucas Books	Friends

RH DIRECT, INC.

Bon Appétit
Gourmet Books
Pillsbury

RH INFORMATION GROUP

Fodor's Travel Publications	Princeton Review
House of Collectibles	RH Español
Living Language	RH Puzzles & Games
Prima Games	RH Reference Publishing

RH INTERNATIONAL (sample from over 100 in thirteen countries)

Areté	RH Mondadori
McClelland & Steward	RH South America

Lt.

Plaza & Janés	RH United Kingdom
RH Autstralia	Transworld UK
RH of Canada Limited	Verlagsgruppe RH

RH LARGE PRINT

WATERBROOK PRESS
Fisherman Bible Study Group
Shaw Books
Waterbrook Press

SIMON & SCHUSTER

SIMON & SCHUSTER AUDIO

Audioworks®	Sound Ideas®
Encore	Success
Pimsleur	

ADULT PUBLISHING GROUP

Atria Books	Simon & Schuster
Kaplan	The Free Press
Pocket Books	The Touchstone and Fireside
Scribner	Group

SIMON & SCHUSTER CHILDREN'S PUBLISHING

Aladdin Paperbacks	S&S Books for Young Readers
Atheneum Books for Young Readers	Simon Pulse
	Simon Spotlight
Little Simon	
Margaret K McElderry Books	

SIMON & SCHUSTER INTERNATIONAL
Simon & Schuster Australia
Simon & Schuster Canada
Simon & Schuster UK

Beyond the Big Five publishing conglomerates are thousands of large, mid-sized and small houses as well as dozens of university presses (UP). UPs publish academic and scholarly nonfiction, art books and literary fiction; some UPs are now also branching into trade nonfiction and fiction. A number of the larger publishing houses, such as Macmillan Books or McGraw-Hill, require submission through an agent; most mid-sized and smaller publishers prefer to deal directly with the author. You can find details about what they want and how they want it in *Writer's Guide to Book Editors, Publishers & Literary Agents* by Jeff Herman (Prima) and Writer's Digest's *Writer's Market* or online at www.pma-online.com, www.booktalk.com and many other sites.

Approach traditional publishers other than the Big Five (HarperCollins, Houghton Mifflin, Penguin Group, Random House and Simon & Schuster) with the same materials you developed to find an agent. Remember, however, that publishers receive an even larger number of submissions every week, so your manuscript, proposal, synopsis and query letter must be in top form before you send it out to your carefully researched list. Landing a traditional publishing contract is difficult and time-consuming, and receiving rejection after rejection on what could end up a one to two or even five to 10 year search can strain the most dedicated writer's nerves.

Authors who do not truly understand how their book is being distributed and where their own responsibilities lie are often dejected by its limited sales and minimal financial return. Plus, in a world where "control" is an issue for so many people, traditional publishing tolerates little or no author input on final editing, design, advertising or distribution, yet requires the author to generate, out of his own pocket, the bulk of promotion. In fact, some publishers expect the author to spend his entire advance on promotion, a turnaround from earlier days when the purpose of the advance was to support the author financially, at least partially, while he worked on his next book. In either case, most advances cover the barest of costs.

Royalties & Advances

Publishing payments as a whole—that is, the relationship between advances and royalties—are often misunderstood. Book contracts allow for a specific advance *against* royalties, with the advance customarily remitted not all at once, but in two or three payments. Typically, the author receives 50% when she signs the contract and 50% either when she sends in two clean copies of the finished manuscript or when the book is actually released. The advance is then *subtracted* from any royalties the author earns until the publisher recoups the full amount already paid out. Only then will she begin receiving additional payments. The higher the advance, the longer the wait until royalty payments begin—and, for many authors, the less likely that royalty earnings will ever equal or exceed the advance. One author with dozens of textbooks to his credit got to the point where he refused to take any advance whatsoever. That way, he always knew how well he was selling. Some publishers will not even send you a statement until your book has sold enough to recover the advance, if ever. Not all publishers offer advances; those who don't expect their authors to wait for their share of the book sales.

Although we hear of the occasional enormous advance paid to a hitherto unknown author, to a celebrity for his autobiography or posthumous exposé or to a prize-winning newcomer, the vast majority of first-book advances from royalty publishers still run in what Publisher's Lunch, a free newsletter put out daily by Cader Books, calls the "nice deal" range, or anything up to $100,000. In similar publishing parlance, a "good deal" advances between $100,001 and $250,000, a "significant deal" tops out at $500,000, and anything greater than $500,001 is listed as a "major deal." Don't let all those big numbers cloud your vision, though; the average first-time author can expect an advance ranging between $500 and $30,000, obviously not enough to live on while writing another book unless the next project can be completed and sold within a matter of a few weeks or months, rather than years. And his chances of selling that next manuscript can be affected by how well he promotes the sale of his first title. If he uses his advance to pay off his Visa bill or buy a new car and limits his promotional activities to local signings, he will likely have a hard time convincing his current or any other publisher to back him again. If, instead, he uses the advance to launch a national or even regional author's tour, hire a publicist, arrange for radio and TV talk shows and press in appropriate magazines and newspapers, all of which advance the sale of his book, his chances of landing that all-important second contract increase significantly. As Chris Gavaler, author of *Pretend I'm Not Here* (Harper Collins, 2002) notes, "Many more first novels are produced each year than second novels, meaning that those whose first books sell poorly often do not get a second chance."

Royalty potential has not changed much in the last few decades. First books from untried, non-celebrity authors still pay in the range of seven to 10% of the wholesale or invoice price. First royalty calculations don't come due for three to six months after a book is released, which can be up 18 months after the publisher accepts it. Since most books do not generate sufficient revenue in the first royalty period to cover the cost of the advance, it can be years before the author receives any additional money—unless he is out there marketing and promoting and generating sales. In contrast, those books that become bestsellers or maintain strong backlist sales can provide their authors with a welcome quarterly or semi-annual revenue.

> ## Did You Know?
> Aviation-thriller author John Nance sued Doubleday and St. Martin's Press for breach of contract after they repeatedly rejected his *Blackout* manuscript, and his upcoming title. The judge noted, however, that the publisher had made many attempts to work with Nance—and ordered him to return the $350,000 advance the publishers had paid him for the two titles.
>
> PW Daily for Booksellers, August 12, 2002

Win the Battle, Lose the War

Many an author has signed a publishing contract only to be disillusioned later, while others have mistakenly turned down what seemed a "useless" offer only to find it was exactly what they needed to open future doors. You must be cognizant of what is and is not customarily available on initial publication—the occasional well-publicized, extravagant first-contract notwithstanding—so you can make an educated decision. Look at an initial contract as the opportunity to launch a career, not retire from one. A typical first contract contains the following agreements and assignments:

> Assign to the publisher the exclusive right to develop, print, translate, publish or cause to be published the full length, condensed, abridged, serialized or adapted versions of the book in all forms and languages, and sell the work in the United States and throughout the world via any and all sales avenues. These forms can include but are not limited to hardcover, paperback, mass market, live or recorded radio or television broadcast, live or recorded stage presentation, video, film, CD, CD-ROM, CD-I, Internet, audio or <u>any other current or future method format</u>.

This is the whole point of the contract, from the publisher's perspective, and is seldom open to negotiation for first-time authors.

> Require from you two complete, double-spaced hard copies of the text plus one copy of each photograph or illustration in final form including any line drawings or diagrams, indices, appendices, forward, introduction and so forth, all at

---

your expense, AND/OR the entire manuscript in digital form via floppy disk.

Failure to deliver by the specified date may be cause to terminate the agreement. In an infamous circumstance toward the end of the 20th Century, HarperCollins cancelled dozens of agreements in one sweep because the authors had not made their contracted deadlines.

Assign to the publisher the right to make any editorial changes, additions or deletions deemed necessary. Proofs of these changes will be available to you; you may be liable for the cost of alterations in type or plates you request in excess of a specified amount (other than printer error). Corrected proofs will probably be presented for inspection at your request only.

This is a deal-breaking clause; if you refuse to allow your work to be amended as the publisher sees fit, the likelihood is he will not publish it at all.

Agree that the publisher may contribute to, delete from, change, revise or correct the work without causing it to be construed as derivative and therefore a new work.

This is the same point as the last clause, only stronger. Not only must you go along with whatever changes the publisher wants, you cannot claim that those changes so materially change the work that it is no longer yours, requires a new contract or infringes on your copyright.

Agree to relinquish your "droit moral," or personal right to protect your expression.

The federal court of appeals in New York called droit moral, "the right of the artist to have his work attributed to him in the form in which he created it." Simply put, if the publisher adds material, takes out sections, revamps the structure, edits to the point of rewrite, lifts sections out of context or in any other way "mangles" your work, you cannot claim your vision has been impugned or demand that your name be removed from the end result. This new clause is actually a hedge against future rights, because as of this writing, the right of droit moral does not legally exist in this country.

Consequently, you may be able to have it deleted from the agreement.

> Assign to the publisher the right to set the price of the book as well as make all decisions regarding format, style, design, editing, production specifications, number of copies printed and pricing.

These are standard publisher rights and, as such, discussible, but seldom negotiable.

> Agree that the publisher will copyright the book in your name in the United States and list it and the appropriate Universal Copyright Convention (U.C.C.) notice in the event the book is published or offered for sale in any other country.

> Agree that the publisher will list notice of copyright for all photographs contained in the book without accepting responsibility for any necessary application, or any possible liabilities for infringement or judgments against individual photographs.

> Agree that if the copyright of the book is infringed and the publisher and author proceed jointly, any expenses and recovery will be shared equally; if the two parties do not proceed jointly, both have the right to proceed alone, committing to the full expense and retaining the full amount of any recovery, regardless of which party holds the copyright.

> Assign the responsibility of originality and liability of content to you, except for that material reprinted with permission. The publisher is held harmless in any claim or suit resulting from the book; you are held responsible for any and all subsequent damages and expenses. If a prepublication legal review of the work finds any part of it unlawful or possibly violating anyone's rights, the publisher has the right to demand you amend the manuscript. If you do not, the publisher can refuse to publish, and demand that you return any and all monies already advanced to you.

This, again, is a deal-breaking issue, so if you are not willing to stand behind your own work, you might as well leave it in a drawer. Publishers carry liability insurance, but plaintiffs have gotten creative with their filings, although they're not necessarily victorious in court. Disgruntled unsuccessful authors charge Copyright Infringement and Plagiarism. Students and cooks claim Error or Omission/Misinformation when chemistry experiments or recipes are missing steps or insufficiently explained. Patients charge False Light when they experience side effects from recommended alternate-health treatments. Celebrities charge Misappropriation of Name/Likeness when their photo is used without their permission. Individuals sue for Public Disclosure of Private Facts or Libel if they feel a character comes too close to home. These cases are often thrown out as nuisance suits or settled out of court, but the cost and trouble of answering them can effectively doom a book and destroy the relationship between author and publisher.

> Agree that the publisher will pay you a specific-percentage royalty of the net sales price—that is, after all discounts, taxes, shipping and customs fees, returns, credits and promotional copies are deducted—on a tiered number of hardcover books, paperback books, mass-market books, audio books and digital books and all other formats. Specific clauses may spell out your royalties on foreign sales, book-club sales, film treatments or scripts and any other applicable medium.

Royalties can sometimes be negotiated, but not usually by the author herself. The best course of action is to accept the royalty schedule and promote the dickens out of the book.

> Agree that the publisher will pay you an advance against these royalties, with a specified amount (normally fifty percent) due on signature of the agreement and another amount due on delivery of the acceptable manuscripts. All payments are made to you as an independent contractor, with the publisher holding no tax payment or withholding liabilities.

> Assign to the publisher the exclusive right to license, sell, or dispose of the rights to the book, with net proceeds divided equally between publisher and you, provided you are given written notice.

> Agree that the publisher will provide you with an accounting of all earnings either quarterly or twice a year, and will

pay any balance within a specified period of time. The publisher may withhold a reasonable reserve for future returns; you may demand to review all bookkeeping records during normal business hours, at your own expense.

Agree that the publisher will provide you with a specified number of copies (anywhere from four to 50) of the book free of charge and will charge you a discounted price, usually the wholesale discount of fifty percent, for additional copies.

This allows you to buy cases of books to sell at the back of the room (BOR) during seminars, presentations and other public appearances, and earn a higher percentage than wholesalers or distributors, because part of their discount must be passed on to the actual bookseller.

Assign the right to the publisher to sell remainder copies (unsold or returned) to whomever the publisher deems advisable, at whatever terms possible.

You will normally receive a percentage, such as 10% of the difference between the publisher's cost and the sales income, if any, in lieu of royalties.

Agree that you will receive no royalties for any free copies of the book in any form, including Braille or audio, given to charities or sent out for promotional purposes.

Agree that all rights will revert to you if the book has been out-of-print with no royalties paid for two consecutive years, provided you request those rights in writing from the publisher and give the publisher six months to make arrangements to reprint.

This clause is the equivalent of a marital prenuptial agreement, in that you hope you will never have to exercise it, but it will protect you in the event the relationship quietly goes sour.

Assign to the publisher the right to discontinue publication at any time. You retain the subsequent right to purchase any existing inventory of sheets and bound stock at cost. All rights covered in the agreement then revert to you.

Agree that the publisher will furnish you with copies of third-party agreements, upon your request.

Assign to the publisher the right to dispose of the original manuscript, proofs and so on, unless requested not to by you in writing.

In today's world, this should not be much of an issue, as you will still have your own saved computer record of both the original and all subsequent changes—provided you've remembered to continually back up your work, of course.

Agree that the publisher will return all photographic materials to you, reimbursing you a set amount for each original if lost or irreparably damaged.

Assign to the publisher the right to deduct all outstanding debts you owe to the publisher from any advance or royalty the publisher owes you.

Assign to the publisher the right to publish your next book, unless terms cannot be agreed upon within 90 days of submission, during which time you cannot submit the manuscript to any other publisher or third party.

This is not a deal-breaking clause, and most literary attorneys advise against it. If your first contract is for a nonfiction but you habitually write fiction, it makes sense to request this clause be deleted. If, on the other hand, you plan to write several more nonfiction books, it can be to your benefit to leave it in. Think about it carefully before you ask to change this standard provision.

Obviously, not all of the above are to your best advantage, but don't distort your publisher's unwillingness to negotiate them as sufficient reason to reject the contract unless you have several publishers clamoring for the same book. Some publishers also stipulate the author's promotional obligations, and may even include the condition that you hire a professional editor within a specified amount of time. For specific advice on making any changes to your initial publishing contract, be sure to ask a *literary* or *intellectual-property* attorney, not an entertainment or general-law attorney.

Self Publishing

The late 20th Century explosion in self-publishing began as a backlash against publisher rejection and/or perceived censorship. Today, self-publishing has grown into a system of highly viable alternatives to royalty publishing for the average author/writer. Financially and emotionally rewarding businesses have grown out of projects initiated with the intention of developing a self-publishing enterprise, although an equal number of people undoubtedly explore this alternative rather than put themselves through the query/rejection process. Before the computer age, self-publishing was usually a euphemism for vanity press. In today's market, desktop prepress, digital-book and POD technology and commercial book manufacturing are leveling the production field, if not the matter of prestige.

Indeed, self-publishing operations no longer suffer from the stigma once associated with their kind, nor do they encounter the immutable resistance to retail distribution that used to be the norm. Thousands of independent retail outlets accept self-published, ISBN-listed books. Even Ingram and Baker & Taylor, the two largest wholesalers in the country, as well as hundreds of distributors and service companies now work with independent and self-publishers, and can be approached inexpensively via affiliation with such organizations as Publishers Marketing Association (PMA) or Small Publishers Association of North America (SPAN). Any self-publisher can join or supply the burgeoning direct-response industry for promotion/sales purposes. The financial potential comes from having no 3rd-party publisher to take the lion's share of the profits. Printing, promoting, marketing, distributing and providing fulfillment for a self-published book, however, demands substantial capital, time and knowledge to be cost effective, much less profitable.

Make no mistake: self-publishing is a demanding, full-time operation, and every success story is matched by at least three to five failures. Only you can decide if, after you've crafted that all-important first book, you want to switch your focus to developing and running a company. Do you want to be an individual who can sit in a quiet room and write, or do you want to spend your days making design and production decisions; pitching your book to middlemen; setting up promotion, publicity and advertising events and materials; handling warehousing, shipping and fulfillment logistics; hiring and overseeing staff—in other words, running a publishing concern? There's a great deal of money to be made in such operations—*just like any other well-run small business.*

In this era of "Home-Based Businesses," you can find information galore on setting up shop, finding financial aid, obtaining all the licenses required, keeping appropriate tax records and so forth in any bookstore, a variety of magazines or at any branch office of the Small Business Administration (SBA). Do not be fooled by the myriad companies and individuals who offer to help you through the process. They make their money **helping people through the process**— not by actually helping you sell your book. You will find few if any service firms, marketing concerns, public-relations houses or book publicists who will work on a commission or "spec" basis, no matter how high a percentage you offer. Plus, if you use one of their ISBNs rather than pay for your own block of numbers, you will **not** be considered the publisher by industry middlemen.

> The entity that owns the ISBN is the publisher of record, and, consequently, the only one with whom distributors, wholesalers and booksellers will conduct business.

Dan Poynter is unquestionably the reigning expert of self-publishing, and you'll find most successful self-publishers have either attended one of his seminars, read his books, or made use of the enormous amount of advice and information available on his website. You will need to keep up with *PW Daily*, at the very least, and join PMA (Publishers' Marketing

Association), SPAN (Small Publishers Association of North America) and SPAWN (Small Publishers, Artists and Writers Network). Current contact information for all of the above can be found via <www.google.com>.

One last word of caution: most small businesses go under within the first five years of opening their doors regardless of how good the product, how dedicated the owner, how small the vision—all due to poor planning. Creating a book through desktop publishing may be far less physically demanding these days, but your efforts will be wasted if you are not prepared to follow up with a flexible, well-financed and well-implemented plan to distribute, market and promote the title.

Vanity/Subsidy Publishing

Vanity presses make their money **publishing the books they sell**. Today, thanks to the lure of hi-tech formats and the amazing number of people with a manuscript in one hand and expendable cash or available credit in the other, the once tiny vanity-press business is swelling at a tremendous rate. Aspiring authors who would never have dreamed of self-publishing ten years ago are now ignoring the discipline necessary to produce a marketable submission and simply plunking down their money to POD publishers, ebook publishers and outright vanity presses who disguise themselves with the euphemism "subsidy." What those authors fail to understand, however, is that regardless of hype, format or proliferation, vanity presses still make their profit from author investment, not from book sales.

If you are paying for the publishing—regardless of what services are being provided or promised—you are, in essence, self-publishing, which is definitely the best course of action for many authors. In recent years, a handful of self-published books such as *The Celestine Prophecy, Looking Out for Number 1* and the first run of *Chicken Soup For The Soul* have attained the kind of public recognition and status usually reserved for traditionally published titles. But note the adjective: a handful. We know about these successes because they are rare enough to be newsworthy. If you convince yourself that your subsidy/vanity publisher is going to make your book into a bestseller, you are spending a lot of money to dash your own dreams. Once the subsidy publisher has your money for the production of the book, *he's made his profit.* You now have to sell enough books to make back the cost of production and the costs you will incur as you market and promote before you see any profit of your own—just as if you'd knowingly self-published. **But**—and it's a really big "But"—you **will not own the ISBN, and therefore cannot control or manipulate your book's distribution.**

Subsidy/Vanity Press means
You <u>Pay</u> All Costs
You <u>Lose</u> All Rights And Control

Acquisition

Acceptance by a vanity press/subsidy publisher is almost guaranteed. Most hold the philosophy that no one has the right to pick and choose who should and shouldn't be in print, and that all authors deserve the chance to have their say. Consequently, unless you submit a novel to a nonfiction-only company or visa versa, in all likelihood any press will take your money and either produce your book or help you do it yourself while you, the author, pay for the production. The press will then include your title in its catalog, put your ebook online or stand by to print POD copies as the orders come in—if **you** cause them to come in.

Beware the Obvious Print

No vanity press calls itself "vanity"; it uses the appealing term "subsidy." And not all subsidy publishers insist on taking the rights to the book; iUniverse.com and Virtual Publishing Group are two popular companies that specifically allow the author to retain all rights. Too many vanity/subsidy publishers, however, do not. The following are typical terms from a vanity/subsidy publisher:

> The author will be paid a royalty of 65% after standard trade discounts for expenses incurred during ongoing promotion (mailing, shipping, etc.)

Besides paying 100% of all production costs, the author also has to pay all promotion, shipping and marketing costs, then give the publisher 35% of whatever is left from every sale. What a deal!

> The publishers have complete publishing and marketing rights for the book for the life of the copyright, or until the publisher returns these rights to the author.

A copyright lasts the life of the author plus 70 years, and the typical contract covers all rights: video, mass market, book clubs, audio, electronic media, foreign sales, etc. No matter what the publishers do—option the book for film, convert it into a documentary, sell it as an ebook, record it as an audio book—the author will continue to have to pay the expenses and lose 35% of the profits to the publisher. If the author wants to make a separate deal for film rights or foreign sales, the publisher still gets his 35%.

> If the book is selling less than 500 copies per annum, the author will accept the return of the remaining inventory in warehouses and will pay the shipping charges.

Since the responsibility to promote and sell the book rests almost entirely on the author except for the publisher's "major efforts," which can amount to nothing more than inclusion in a catalog mailing, press releases and a few book signings at local Barnes & Nobles, the author could easily end up with 1,000 copies of his book—at 40 to a carton, upwards of 30 pounds per box—piled in his garage or sitting in his living room.

All at his own expense, of course.

Did You Know?

The data for the various bestseller lists is taken from sales figures provided by various sources. For example, Amazon.com's bestseller list is internal, as is BarnesandNoble.com's. *Booksense Bestsellers* is based on reports from independent bookstores across the country. *Boston Globe Bestsellers* is based on figures from Barnes & Noble, Borders Books & Music, Brookline Booksmith, Harvard Book Store, Lauriat's/Royal Discount, Rizzoli, Waterstone's and WordWorth. *Los Angeles Times* lists are based on sales in the Southern California area. The *New York Times Bestseller List* indicates sales figures in New York.

10
The Process

Prepress
Prepress comprises the **final edit/proofing** that brings a project in line with the publisher's style; **design**, which includes interior text formatting, illustration layout and cover design; **title selection**; **price setting** and **scheduling/costing** and obtaining the appropriate **registrations**. Except for editing, the bulk of this section is for the self-publisher or the author who wants to take an active part in the subsidy/vanity press. Traditional publishers retain all rights and control over prepress matters.

Editing

Although most large houses expect their purchased manuscripts to come in fully developed and editorially clean, they may still amend those manuscripts in keeping with their internal style guide. Some houses, for example, spell out all numbers—four; seventeen; one hundred; thirty-five—some spell out only ten and below, some only use digits. Other possible style-guide issues include list commas (1, 2, and 3 or 1, 2 and 3), punctuation with quotes (inside, "Hi, there," or outside, "Hi, there",) chapter breaks, page headers and so on.

Furthermore, remember that books are not just personal to their authors and readers, but also to the agents who represent them and the editors who buy them. Many editors like to put their "thumb print" on the books they acquire. Some feel that all first-time authors need extensive editing to bring their work up to professional standards, be it the house's or their own. Others simply give in to the most powerful force in the world: the urge to alter someone else's writing. Expect to continue the editing process with your traditional publisher until the manuscript satisfies both of you—or at least him.

Smaller publishers may actually line-edit their purchased titles, sometimes even to the point of ghostwriting, if the author has the correct credentials and the book covers a topic they want to include on their list. In this sense, they carry out all traditional publishing functions. On the downside, of course, they cannot afford to pay the same advance figures as larger publishers who expect the material to be ready on final submission.

All this begs the question: if publishers go to such lengths to edit the work they buy, why are so many sloppily edited books released every year? Perhaps, as one professional editor who prefers to remain nameless put it, not everyone knows how to do their job as well as you might hope or expect. Ergo, the responsibility once again falls on you, the author: the best way to avoid over-editing, sloppy editing or erroneous editing during the stage of the process in which you have the least control is to ensure your structure is flawless, your thesis or story fully developed and your copy crisp, compelling and error-free.

Self-publishers should pass their work in front of at least one professional "cold eye" to ensure they've written what they think they've written. Vanity/subsidy presses may edit your work either for an extra fee or as part of their package deal. If you pay for it separately, you do not have to accept those editorial changes with which you disagree; if editing is part of your package contract, you may have signed away that right.

Book Design

Designing a book means **formatting** the text, chapter openings, headers, page numbers, footnotes, table of contents, index and appendices, if any; choosing the various **font** styles and sizes; determining the odd/even page **headers**; **positioning** the text and illustrations and creating the **cover**. Traditional and vanity/subsidy publishers provide these services as part of their publishing contracts, often using the same photo, graphics and page-layout programs available to self-publishers. Even if your heart does not go all aflutter at the idea of pouring over font charts or you are visual-esthetics challenged, you can end up with a beautiful hardcover or paperback trade volume worthy of sitting on any bookstore's shelf; an entire service industry of graphic designers, cover artists, design-and-print houses and POD designer/printers has sprung up to produce polished, market-ready products within a reasonable budget on a limited time table. Although the decisions are still many and the cost significant, thanks to 21st century technology, book design is now a relatively carefree task. The following, therefore, is merely a guide to the vernacular involved in this production phase.

Illustrating

All books require **cover design**; many also require **line art**, **special artwork**, and/or **photographs**. Self-publishers must provide or obtain all artwork. Traditionally published authors are responsible for providing everything except the cover design and the pictures in children's books; most publishers prefer to use their own illustrators. You must obtain permission from the owner or artist to use any photographs or artwork you do not originate.

> **Line art** is anything not comprising dots that can be printed as if text. It must be black and white with no shades of gray. Computer-generated "drawn" graphics and pen-and-ink illustrations are line art. **Special artwork** can be an illustration generated either by a non-"drawing" computer program or by

an artist in materials other than pen-and-ink. It may or may not be in color. Standard click art is special artwork. **Digital photographs** reproduce best; let your printer or designer scan your processed photographs onto disk unless you have a high-resolution scanner.

Cover design refers to the front and back cover of the bound book plus the spine, and encompasses any device, pattern or picture shown as well as the type, style and placement of the title, publisher, ISBN, back-cover text, bar coding and so forth. "You can't judge a book by its cover" is a great saying but it's also a myth; covers and titles can make or break any book. Reps carry cover mock-ups and flyers rather than books. Bookstore browsers look at the title, the front cover, and the back cover blurbs, how the pages are laid out, how strongly the first paragraph of the first chapter grabs them and the price. Catalog and book-club consumers base their decisions on the title, the front cover, the blurb, any one-line review that might be added and, of course, the price. If the title and/or cover art does not grab the reader immediately, chances are the rest of the criteria will never be noticed. If you are self-publishing, therefore, you must know the different artistic elements available, as well as the processes involved in utilizing them.

Different types of artists perform different functions. Graphic artists or designers can typically provide the line art needed for diagrams, specifications, image reproductions and covers. Illustrators produce visualization of thought, such as scenes from a science-fiction novel or pictures in a children's book. Look for them in *Literary Market Place*; at art or design studios; through local art guilds, museums, institutes or schools; in advertising agencies or print shops; or through an internet search.

Title Selection

Since a title can, by itself, boost sales or doom a book to oblivion, choose yours carefully. Most nonfiction has two titles: a few eye-catching words followed by a subtitle that tells what the book is about. Clarity is as important as being catchy and a positive inclination sells better than a negative one. "How To" titles are strong for selling through mail order or direct mail. Action words add vigor if used appropriately, but remember that "ing" verbs are not necessarily active.

Fiction is more difficult to title. The author's sense of what is inside the novel must be brought into play, as well as a feeling for what constitutes the pivotal point, character, scene or object. Fiction titles can be intriguing, mysterious or enlightening. Vanity/subsidy fiction seldom sells more than a few dozen copies and self-published fiction is an upward battle. Traditional publishers will have their own ideas about what to title your book.

Pricing

Conventional wisdom claims that the retail price of a trade paper-and-ink book should be 8 times its production cost, although most mass-market books generally sell at a lower percentage. Ebooks are loosely priced at what the market will allow; audio books have to take into account the cost of the actor who records the book and higher reproduction expenses. When pricing your own book, first calculate the cost of printing and shipping, then find out the price-range of your competition.

Only consider the print run and shipping charges when you calculate the production cost, not the expense of design, illustrating, promoting, advertising and so forth. Since soft-cover books must have the price printed on the outside cover, you'll need to estimate the final expense, multiple by eight, adjust to the competition's price, then lift or lower to the nearest $.95, a retail pricing standard.

If you are pricing a book strictly for direct marketing, the above guidelines need not apply. The cost of a direct-marketed title is less important to the consumer than the information, provided the book offers what the reader wants to know; hence, the value of the material dictates its price. Books marketed via television P.I. (per inquiry) ads and infomercials may sell well at $49.95, or even $159.95 when the same book would not move in a trade store if priced over $19.95. Remember, though, this exception applies only to nonfiction titles sold exclusively by direct marketing—and not, curiously, on the Internet, where people expect bargains or at least reasonable prices. Titles included in catalogs and book clubs must be competitive at least within the catalog. Titles available in bookstores or other catalogs must be competitive with the general market.

Audio books are more expensive to produce, so they cost more to buy, starting at a retail price of $24.95 and going up to $49.95 or even $69.95 for larger books. CDs are considerably less expensive to produce, so their retail prices range from $5.95 to $29.95. The expense of an ebook is in creating the digital file, not in producing a tangible product; consequently, ebooks sell from $1.95 up to $19.95, but seldom beyond.

The public-at-large has a psychological inhibition about paying over $10, $20 or $25 for a paper-and-ink book. If a book can be priced $8.95 or $9.95, price it at $9.95; if the decision is between $9.95 and $10.95, leave it at $9.95; if it comes down to $23.95 or $25.95, go with the more comfortable $24.95. You'll find exceptions to these rules everywhere; this is only a guide. Specific-target books can be priced slightly higher, while general trade books need to stay toward the low end.

Another quirk most consumers share is an aversion to "buying cheap." Don't be the lowest-priced book among a field of competitors, which means any book on the same subject or on a different subject but within the same category or of the same type. For example, titles competitive with a hardcover biography of John Lennon would be other hardcovers about John Lennon, other hardcover biographies, or hardcovers of a similar subject such as the music business.

The only other rule to remember is that a mass of exceptions exists for all these rules.

When pricing your self-published book, remember that wholesalers, distributors and booksellers buy at a 20-65% discount depending upon the terms of the sale. An author's royalties are normally calculated as a percentage of the wholesale or invoice price, so a direct sale to a bookstore at a 30% discount will net a higher royalty than a sale via a wholesaler who gets a 50% discount. On the other hand, the bookstore may only buy one or two copies at a time, while the wholesaler may buy dozens or even cases at a time.

Costing/Scheduling

When you request a price quote (Request for Quote, or RFQ) from a book manufacturer or POD printer, include the width and height of the book, the total number of pages, the weight of paper you want, the number of pages with color, the number of photographs or special artwork if not already included in a graphics file, whether the cover is one-, two- or four-color and the type of binding. Ask for price breaks on a range of copies (100, 500, 1,000, 5,000, 10,000, etc.), how long the project will take (production time) and the printer's availability. Send RFQs to at least five to 20 printers; prices may vary greatly. Printers customarily expect to be paid ½ up front and ½ before they ship. Schedule the official release of the book for three to four months <u>after</u> you take delivery of the books so you have time to implement your marketing plan and get your book out to reviewers, who prefer to publish their reviews before the title is released.

Registrations

Copyright

All published books, including those self-published, need to be registered with the Library of Congress Copyright Office. Most fiction and nonfiction books are copyrighted on Form TX, Nondramatic Literary Works; full instructions are included with each application. If you are being published, your publisher will handle this for you; you need not register your copyright before publication. If you are self-publishing, you can obtain an application form by writing or calling the Library of Congress Copyright Office or going to their website at http://www.loc.gov/copyright/. A copy of the completed work must be deposited in the Library of Congress along with the application and a $30 fee (as of this writing). Depositing this material is a safeguard against other people claiming the material as their own, not an act of copyrighting in itself. **All creative works are automatically copyrighted from the time they are produced, but without registration of the final version, your proof of creation and ownership can be challenged.** Thirty dollars is a pittance weighed against the time, expense and heartache of defending an unregistered copyright.

Copyright protects the *literal and exact duplication* of a document, all the way down to the paragraph level. What it does **not** protect are ideas, information, titles or statistical data; these cannot be copyrighted. Ergo, a writer who "lifts" material from another work, being careful to reword each sentence and paragraph, is technically not infringing on the original copyright. At that point, the question is one of ethics or financial accountability, which usually requires a judge's opinion. The famous case of Art Buchwald, for example, claiming he created the story behind Eddie Murphy's "Coming to America" was not a matter of copyright infringement, but of plagiarism.

The copyright notice must be placed "on all publicly distributed copies from which the work can be visually perceived." List it on the copyright page, known as the verso (other side) of the title page. This leaf also contains the name of the publisher and distributor (if applicable), a rights clause, the ISBN, LCCN, CIP number (if applicable) and any independent network's access point number.

A **rights clause** defines the copyright, typically stating something along the lines of: "All rights reserved. No part of this book may be reproduced in any form or by any means, electronic or mechanical, including photocopying, recording or by any information storage and retrieval system, without written permission from the publisher." Wording may vary.

Access-point numbers are automated catalog referral numbers. They allow librarians to locate a specific book even if the title, subtitle, format (hardcover to paperback), or author byline has changed. ISBN (International Standard Book Number) and LCCN (Library of Congress Card Number) are two universal access-point numbers, both of which are now available on automated catalogs. Independent networks servicing libraries often use their own access-point numbers.

ISBN

The International Standard Book Number (ISBN) is a reference identification system designed to reduce the confusion inherent in a business where titles, authors, and publishers may have similar or even identical names. An ISBN is unique to one title or edition of a title from one specific publisher. Each format of a book requires a separate ISBN: paperback, hardcover, ebook, audio book, CD-ROM and so forth. Each title in a series needs a separate ISBN; the series as a whole requires an ISSN, International Standard Serial Number, as does any title published annually.

ISBNs can never be reassigned or reused. Any book sold through industry middlemen or retail booksellers must have an ISBN. For $225.00, RR Bowker will provide any publisher with 10 ISBNs; $350 will get them to you via Express Mail. ISBNs are not offered individually.

In addition to appearing on the copyright page, the ISBN is also bar-coded on the lower right-hand corner of the outside back cover and/or back jacket. Paperback books can also include the ISBN on the spine of the book. If a price is printed with the ISBN, there must be two spaces between the ISBN and price code. Although a new ISBN must be assigned for every new edition or format change, the original ISBN is maintained during price changes.

R.R. Bowker originated and controls these reference systems, along with reference systems for music (International Standard Music Number, or ISMN) and other material goods (Standard Address Number, or SAN). Bowker's site, http://www.bowker.com, is also a good resource for bar-code suppliers, printers, POD referrals, and other Bowker products and services, such as *Books in Print* and bookwire.com.

LCCN

The Library of Congress Control Number (LCCN) is the second primary access-point-number system used in the United States. LCCNs are used for authority, bibliographic and classification records, which highlight exactly what kind of material the book contains and where it would be found in the Library of Congress. The LCCN normally appears on the copyright page only, and is not required in any other location.

Libraries seldom purchase books that do not have LCCNs. You can obtain yours through the Library of Congress' PCN (Preassigned Control Number) Program at http://pcn.loc.gov/pcn/ (note: no "www"), but it must be done before publication. LCCNs are not available for titles published outside the U.S., for serials, ebooks, government documents, booklets (under 50 pages), textbooks below the college level, mass-market paperbacks, audiovisual materials and a number of other book types. Check the website for eligibility and the application process.

ABI

When you send for an ISBN, Bowker will send you an Advance Book Information (ABI) Form, which lets you list your book in *Forthcoming Books In Print* and *Books in Print*, two of the most important directories in the industry. The latter is the first-try reference for all researchers, librarians, etc., who want to find a volume by subject, title or author. Listings are free to the author or publisher and may also be included in the smaller, specialized directories published by Bowker services.

Detailed instructions accompany the forms; read them carefully, as some terminology may be unfamiliar. Forms should be completed approximately six months before release of the book, provided the release date is reasonably fixed. Bowker will then provide a checklist every other month or so for updating. Complete and return these checklists each time to ensure your listing is included accurately in the annual directory. The form has sufficient room for a description of the book as well as a brief projection of marketing tactics. Copies of the completed form are often used for promotional purposes as part of advance-notice presentations.

CIP

Cataloging in Publication (CIP) is a block of information on the verso that offers librarians a starting point for categorizing an individual book. The free LC-CIP is prepared by the

Library of Congress (LC) for those publishers who have published at least three books (by at least three different authors) likely to be acquired by U.S. libraries. The process is slow and the volume great; in March, 2003 the Library of Congress' website acknowledged it was just receiving mail dating back to fall, 2001.

Libraries seldom buy books that do not have this vital block of information. New publishing houses, self-publishers and publishers with tight schedules can take matters into their own hands and create a "Publisher's Cataloging in Publication" or P-CIP. Do not attempt to create this on your own without a librarian's help or advice. Quality Books Inc, a library middleman, provides P-CIP^{SM} for a modest fee. Find them at http://www.quality-books.com/qb_pcip2.html.

Production

In the final publishing phase, paper books are set up for print, duplicated, assembled and bound. Ebooks are formatted into PDF or LIT files and burned onto CDs or uploaded onto the Internet. Audio books are recorded and duplicated. Each format has its own process.

Paper Books

Whether manufactured or printed on demand, a book's production cost depends on the number of pages, the size and shape of the volume, the weight and type of paper used, the cover style and material, the extent of internal color, the type of binding and the number of copies run. Both manufacturers and printers will still work off camera-ready hard copies (printed pages) but prefer formatted disks. Both will help with layout, if necessary, scan in photographs and line or black-and-white artwork and create digitized separations of color artwork. Once the entire work is completely digitized, however, the two methods diverge.

Manufacturing

A book manufacturer runs the files through an image-setter, which imposes the images onto film. From the resulting negatives, the pages are stripped into signatures (sigs), which are reproduced into bluelines and shown to the publisher for final correction, then burned onto aluminum plates. Printing technology is advancing daily; some manufacturers can now burn plates directly from disk and offer their publishers digital proofs rather than paper bluelines.

> **Stripping** refers to the placement of each negative onto a flat sheet, to compose or lay out the sig for platemaking. **Sigs**, or signatures, are the sheets that run through the press. The pages are laid out on sigs in multiples of eight: sixteen, thirty-two, sixty-four and so on. A sixteen sig, for example, will fold into sixteen book pages. **Bluelines** are copies made of the stripped negatives, before the plates are made. Blueline sheets, the size of the sigs, are folded to appear as the book will appear, so the publisher can see how it will look. A blueline is exactly like the final print, except for the ink color.

Once approved, the plates are prepared or burned, mounted on a sheet-fed or web printing press, and offset.

> **Burning the plates** is the process of making an aluminum or plastic plate from which to print. Plates are reproduced using the stripped negatives. Sheet-fed printing feeds sheets the size of the sig through the machine to be printed onto. **Web printing** feeds a continuous sheet from a huge roll of paper. Web printing is faster and less expensive for long runs, but far more costly for short runs. It should only be used for extremely large print runs, in the tens of thousands. Sheet-fed printing is used for most books. **Offset printing**, one of the most common methods of modern printing, is accom-

plished by a right-reading plate offsetting the type onto a rubber blank backwards, or wrong-reading, which then offsets the type forward, or right-reading, onto the paper. Most books are sheet-fed through an offset printer.

Colored pages are run on a four-cylinder or unit press with each cylinder printing one of the process colors. Once all the pages have been printed, the sigs are assembled and bound. If the book is soft-covered, the cover is bound with the sigs.

A **perfect-bound** book has been folded and gathered with the binding edge ground off to leave a rough surface. Adhesive and a special lining are applied over the spine (binding edge); the covers are then glued into place. A **stitched** or **saddle-stitched** book has been stapled through the backbone, allowing it to lie flat when opened. Although magazines, newsletters, some catalogs and small booklets use saddle stitching, it is impractical for a full-length novel or nonfiction book. **Comb binding** or **GBC** is the plastic equivalent of wire-spiral binding. **Deluxbinding** is a softcover substitute for Smythe sewing. It begins as perfect binding. Cheesecloth is then applied to the back of the ground sigs; the cover is glued to the sides only, not to the cheesecloth. In this way, a softcover book can be bound in a similar fashion to a hardcover. **Smythe sewing** is the strongest and most durable type of binding. The signatures are individually saddle stitched, then linked to each other by thread. The front and back pages are then glued to the insides of the front and back soft cover or hard case. Smythe-sewn books open flat and do not "break," which is one of the hazards of perfect bound books.

POD

POD printers can offer their proofs online if you like, and can make changes even to final proofs without extra charge. Because they use high-speed laser printers to print individual pages, just like a desktop printer, they can also make changes between runs. Pages that include color are run on a four-color printer, and hi-gloss covers are run on special machines kept in atmosphere-controlled rooms. The pages are then assembled and bound.

POD binding is similar to manufactured perfect binding in that adhesive and a special binding are applied to the edges and the cover glued over them. Typically, in fact, the binding is the only difference discernable to the average reader between a POD volume and a manufactured one. Since a POD book has no sigs, the pages are merely pressed together one after the other and, as such, can be torn out of the book one page at a time. To avoid this, the better POD printers will extend the binding around the front and back edges. Unfortunately that means the book can never open quite as fully as a perfect-bound volume without taking the risk of a page or two coming loose.

Ebooks

The trick to producing an ebook is in designing/formatting the entire work into one long, continuous file from stem (cover) to stern (index), rather than into a number of files that can be separately processed. At that point, the work is converted into an ebook format and either burned onto a master compact disk (CD) or uploaded onto a website for immediate sale via downloading. CDs can be reproduced for a fraction of a paper book, and the publisher can choose to impose digital right management (DRM) protections so the file cannot be printed, copied or altered. Microsoft Ebook Readers can also download a program that lets the reader "speak" the ebook text via a synthesized voice.

Ebook technology continues to advance. Originally, Adobe PDF was the only viable eBook format. Then came the Microsoft LIT format and the Gemstar eBook format. Now we have the similar-to-mp3 format for the multi-functional hiebook (a hand-held reader), the hypertext format with chapter-indexed links for Instant eBooks, simple MS Word formatting for reading off any computer, and the Mo-bipocket Reader Format for PDAs, Palm Readers, Windows CE, Pocket PC and so forth. If you bought this book more than fifteen minutes ago, no doubt other formats and Readers are already available.

While most experts agree ebooks are unlikely to replace paper books, they are an addition that, according to an Association of American Publishers (AAP) study, lead consumers to purchase the book in other formats as well. Statistics vary; some experts claim ebooks account for only .10% (one-tenth of one percent) of all book sales, while individual publishers point to a 30% or higher figure, at least for their own companies. Internet connections within bookstores, both at Information Booths and on the floor for consumers to use, link the various formats available for a given title, and hence encourage the maximum sale of the book.

Audio Books

Audio books involve at the very least a direct-to-disk recording system, a director/producer and an actor or reader who can, over the course of a number of sessions, read the entire text articulately and with enthusiasm. Most audio books do not incorporate music, but those that do include it during the editing stage, after which the recording is burned onto a master CD. The master then goes to a duplication house, which reproduces it onto CDs or cassette tapes. With the right equipment, knowledge and speaking talent, an author can produce an audio book in her living room, outsource the package graphics to a design shop and the duplication to a hi-speed dupe house, and have a viable product within a matter of a week or two.

All she has to do is come up with the cash or credit.

11
Going To Market

The final phase of a book's life involves three separate, yet overlapping campaigns: **distribution, marketing, promotion** plus the functions of **fulfillment**. Each campaign is a full-time occupation, with few clear-cut lines between who does what, and where one function ends and another starts. In fact, a cursory glance at the myriad alternatives available causes a sense of futility in the uninitiated, especially since many active industry participants and advisors are themselves confused about who, what, why and how things are done in the distribution and marketing spheres. You cannot even count on every marketing department or company to handle the same functions, in fact, since some focus on distribution and promotion while others confine themselves to publicity and advertising. The terminology matters less than finding the right people to get the book into the hands of as many readers as possible. Whether you are self-publishing, being traditionally published, or handing over your money to a subsidy publisher, you need to know what is going on with your book, and take steps to fill in where others are not planning or producing what you want.

Distribution

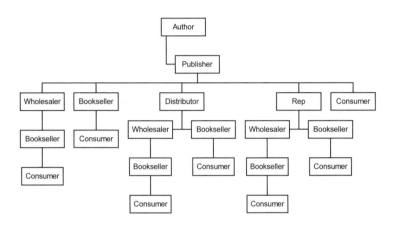

Distribution is the routes or methods by which a book is physically moved from the printer's or publisher's warehouse to or in front of the buying public. As with any product, this can be accomplished in a variety of ways. The book business has **seven routes of distribution** with **four possible layers of middlemen** between the publisher and the consumer: wholesalers, distributors, reps/brokers and booksellers.

> ## Did You Know?
>
> A number of publishing houses also distribute for smaller publishers, which means they send the titles of the smaller house into the same distribution chain as their own titles. HCI, for example, which has been in the recovery book business for decades but made its biggest mark by publishing the *Chicken Soup for the Soul* series, now provides sales, marketing, warehousing and fulfillment for the Hazeldon Foundation, which also produces recovery books.

Wholesalers buy from the publisher at a 50% discount, warehouse the books and fill orders from booksellers. The two largest wholesalers in the country are Ingram and Baker & Taylor (B&T), both of which have multiple divisions, including POD publishing and distributor services. Both can be approached by small and even self-publishers via special programs available to Publishers Marketing Association (PMA) members; they generally accept all books whose publishers meet their criteria. Most retail booksellers will not stock a book if Ingram, Baker & Taylor or one of the smaller wholesalers doesn't carry it. Wholesalers pay their invoices "net 90," which means three months after they have received the merchandise.

Distributors represent a publisher's entire catalog and actively pitch directly to booksellers or libraries. They take books on consignment rather than buying outright, take on only those new publishers whose catalogs have been carefully reviewed and expect exclusive distribution rights. They bundle less popular books with high-profile ones, and usually pay 90 or more days after the closing date for sales in any given month.

A **publisher's catalog** includes all the books being actively sold in all formats: hardcover, paperback, mass market, audio and digital in its various forms. Hence, the term refers both to the titles and the physical booklet listings. The different tiers within a catalog are the Frontlist, or those titles released since the previous catalog for the present season, and the Backlist, those titles still in the publisher's catalog from a previous season. Traditionally, the book industry has been a two-season cycle: spring and fall, but today most publishers include a third season over the summer. A spring-release title still listed in the fall is part of the backlist, as is a title that has continued to sell for a number of years. Many smaller publishers disregard the traditional seasons and revise their catalogs as books are released.

Bundling is the practice of including copies of secondary titles along with a popular one. When a store orders 50 copies of the latest bestseller, for example, it may also receive four copies of three or four other titles as part of the deal, or to fill up the case. This is an important practice for authors to understand, because if a book is not slated for major promotion it may get into most of its outlets through bundling. If so, even if the copies sell off the shelves quickly the title will probably not be reordered unless the bookseller experiences a demand for it.

Reps/brokers are individual or groups of salespeople who perform the same function as distributors, but on a non-exclusive basis.

Consumers are the final buyers, and include the **public**, or individual readers; **educational institutions** such as elementary, secondary and trade schools, community and four-year colleges, universities and special-focus academies such as art, music and dance institutes; publicly or privately owned **libraries**; and **commercial buyers** such as businesses, hospitals or corporations that buy books for their own use rather than for resale.

Booksellers

Booksellers include the vast network of over 4,000 independent **trade bookstores** that belong to the American Booksellers Association (ABA), and the tens of thousands of bookstores that sell English-language books and/or their translations around the world. They buy on a scheduled discount and sell at or slightly below retail.

Each publisher, distributor and wholesaler has its own, but a standard discount schedule might read:

Single copy	20%	200 or more	45%
2-49 copies	30%	College bookstores	30%

50-99 copies	35%	Libraries	20%
100-199 copies	40%		

In today's crossbreed world, few independent bookstores can afford to sell only new, paper-format books. Most also carry audio and ebooks as well as ancillary products such as calendars, eReaders and so on. Many used-book stores, such as Bookman in Orange County, California, also have a web presence <ebookman.com> and offer rare and out-of-print search-and-broker services. Trade stores showcase bestsellers and new releases with POP displays.

> **POP** or **point-of-purchase** displays are table and life-size stand-up poster/racks that hold a limited number of book copies. The display focuses readers' attention on the title, which is also shelved in conspicuous locations throughout the store as well as in the expected alphabetical or subject position.

Barnes & Noble (B&N), the largest **chain bookseller** in the country, crosses the line between retailer, wholesaler and publisher. As a retailer, B&N has 900-plus bookstores and 1,186 GameStop video and entertainment software stores; any publisher or author can submit directly to have B&N carry its title(s) in both the brick-and-mortar stores and on <barnesandnoble.com>. Like a wholesaler, B&N stocks most of the inventory for those 2,000-plus stores in its own warehouses. And its publishing arm, Barnes & Noble Publishing, reprints classic titles, "lifestyle" and coffee-table books, plus an imprint, Folio Editions, for "individual portfolios of photographs or illustrations on singular subjects." In 2003, B&N acquired Sterling Publishing, a crafts, hobby, gardening and how-to niche publisher, to broaden B&N's title distribution beyond its own chain of stores. As of this writing B&N Publishing is also expanding into literary novels—and who knows what else tomorrow. B&N creates its own POP displays to highlight those titles it wants to push and to advertise its schedule of in-store author appearances. The company even offers Barnes and Noble University, which offers free and fee-based online classes in a variety of subjects, all taught by experts in their field. From being a small chain among thousands of bookstores, Barnes and Noble has grown to be a major power in the 21st Century book industry. No author, publisher, publicist, wholesaler, distributor or rep can afford to ignore it.

Internet bookstores, which number in the tens if not hundreds of thousands, come in two flavors: straight booksellers that sell books in all formats just like a brick-and-mortar store, and hybrids, like Jeff Bezo's Amazon.com. Bezo's highly successful experiment orders books on consignment like a distributor, expects a 50-55% discount like a wholesaler, sells directly to the consumer at retail or slightly discounted retail prices like Barnes & Noble and Borders, offers used books and search services like a broker and provides warehousing and online services for **Borders Books and Music**, the second-largest chain bookseller in the country. In contrast, **Bookzone.com** buys from wholesalers and publishers like a traditional bookstore, sells discounted versions of popular books in hardcover, paperback, ebook and audio, and provides used, rare and out-of-print book search-and-broker services.

Membership warehouses buy in large volume at wholesale or greater discount, then distribute the books to their various outlets where they are put out on long tables to be leafed through and handled for approximately six weeks. At the end of the sales window, the warehouse returns the unsold copies to the publisher or wholesaler for full invoice credit, even though many of the returns are too dirty or damaged to be resold. Membership warehouses justify this procedure with the size of their orders, but many small publishers feel the one-two punch of high discounts and damaged returns negates that benefit.

Display Marketers are high-volume booksellers that buy books in quantities of 10,000 to 250,000 or more and sell them at deep discounts through marketing events to **corporations**, **universities**, **early learning centers**, **hospitals**, **government offices** and **non-profit organizations**. There are only a handful of these companies in the US, Canada and United Kingdom, but they help put many books, including *Chicken Soup For the Soul* and *Men Are From Mars, Women Are From Venus,* on the bestseller lists. Their buyers don't care how large or small the publisher is, but they already have relationships with the larger houses, which all have full-time staff devoted to selling to this and other non-traditional markets. Consequently, they don't always notice individual submissions. Small and self-publishers should pitch their titles through a distributor or rep/broker.

Specialty outlets include music stores, health-food stores, home-and-garden shops, card shops, auto-supply stores, computer stores, office-supply stores, museum and hospital gift shops, children's stores and any other type of outlet that carries books to support its primary merchandise.

Book clubs also buy in bulk and sell at a discount, but their returns are seldom damaged. Some book clubs buy the right to produce their own version of the title rather than sell the publisher's. The club's edition usually has a less-expensive cover and a larger page size, which thus reduces the cost per copy and allows them to make a higher profit selling at a lower price.

Book Catalogs are booklets published by direct mail booksellers who advertise other publisher's titles. These titles are bought outright, held on consignment, or purchased on a per-order basis and drop-shipped to the consumer.

Mass markets are both a specific type of outlet—supermarkets, drug stores, convenience stores and so on—and the particular version of titles usually carried in those stores. Formerly called pocket books or dime novels, mass-market editions of bestselling books are approximately four inches wide by seven inches tall. They are normally displayed cover out rather than spine out, and are designed to fit on both magazine/book racks within the store and on impulse-buy racks at the checkstands.

Backorder refers to books that have been ordered by booksellers or wholesalers, but cannot be delivered because the publisher is out of stock and the new shipment has not yet arrived from the printer.

Out-of-print means the publisher no longer lists the book in its catalog and will not be ordering any new copies from the printer. Unsold copies still in the printer's, publisher's or wholesaler's warehouses are called **remainders**.

2nd printing means the initial run of copies has sold out and more duplications of the exact same plates or files have been ordered from the printer.

Reprint refers to re-releasing a book that has been out-of-print and is being re-released under a different publisher's imprint. In other writing markets, reprint refers to the resale of the exact same article in different magazines. Reprint can also refer to the right to quote material from another published source; in this case, written permission must be obtained from the author and/or publisher first.

Revised means the book has been printed again with the text updated, corrected or in some way altered. This makes it a new edition, requiring a new ISBN.

Returns are books sent back to the publisher because they are not moving. Publishers must expect some returns, regardless of which distribution route(s) they employ.

Reissues are books that have been out-of-print and are now being printed for sale again by the original publisher. Often, when authors have a bestseller with their third or fourth book, the publisher will reissue the first two or three titles to take advantage of the author's new popularity.

The Campaign

A distribution campaign needs to address all four types of middlemen and all types of booksellers to take advantage of the tens-of-thousands of potential distribution points that will put a given title in front of its hundreds-of-millions of potential readers. Not all distribution points are viable for all books, of course, but a publisher who confines himself to only one or two is as shortsighted and naïve as the author who believes a subsidy/vanity press' catalog mailings to a few hundred or even thousand bookstores is effective distribution. Persuading the various middlemen and booksellers to carry a particular book requires a well-crafted marketing campaign backed up with the appropriate materials and dynamic author promotion.

Self-publishers need to create this plan themselves, but even traditionally published authors should sit down with their publisher's marketing departments and find out who is going to warehouse their book, who is going to pitch it and to whom they're going to pitch. If your publisher's distributor is not going to cover all the distribution points you envision, draw up your own plan and either ask the company to work with you, or implement it yourself. After all, it is **your book.**

Did You Know?

According to SCB Distributors, Los Angeles is the largest book market in the country, outdistancing second-place New York by more than $50 million each year.

Marketing

A well-crafted **marketing** campaign creates a public demand for the book by putting the title and author in front of the media and thus inducing booksellers to order it, wholesalers to stock it and distributors and reps to peddle it. Traditional publishers have two independent departments for promoting their titles: publicity and marketing. **Publicity** is the free media coverage provided in response to a promotional event (such as the release of the book), or a newsworthy circumstance (such as a review). Publicity can also be a feature article that employs quotes from the book or its author. Blurbs gained through publicity can then be used in other promotional campaigns. The publicity department, therefore, works on getting the book reviewed, getting the author print and broadcast interviews and getting both the book and author included in feature stories.

The **Marketing** department concentrates on two high-cost areas, advertising and direct mailings. **Advertising** is paid solicitation aimed at specific clusters that can be geared either to inform the public of the book's existence or a special event, or to produce a direct sale by mail order or per inquiry (P.I.). **Direct mailings,** while effective if well targeted, are also quite costly and time-consuming. Ergo, postcards are usually sent only to the author's own contact list unless the author is willing to handle the direct mailing campaign himself.

> **Cluster** is a market-research term for the classification of people according to spending habits, income, and interests. Clusters can be subdivided or grouped and their locations mapped geographically. Sophisticated market research techniques, such as PRIZM, an indexing system from Claritas based on zip codes, can locate and map the approximately 6.3 million people who buy nonfiction hardcovers annually, providing valuable information as to where

and through what publications a specific book should be marketed. Determining the correct cluster(s)—and consequent correct advertising vehicles and bookselling outlets—is the main thrust behind any marketing plan.

Mail order, also colloquially known as **direct marketing**, refers to sales made from advertising in magazines, newspapers, etc. or orders placed in response to ads sent through the mail, seen on TV, or heard on the radio. **Direct mailing** is exactly what the name implies: sending postcards, flyers or letters to every name on a mailing list, usually rented, of people who have bought or shown an interest in similar titles. Those who buy can then be counted as customers, and, as such, can be added to the sender's in-house mailing list. Those who do not respond to the mailing cannot be solicited again without the sender paying another rental fee for the list.

Per-inquiry, or **P.I.**, is the kind of advertising that commands TV viewers or radio listeners to "call now." P.I. is most effective when called into a toll-free number.

Special events are reasons to buy immediately, such as sales, special price reductions or new shipments.

Every title requires tailored materials—bound galleys, postcards and flyers, flat covers, book folios, press kits and a written marketing plan—to implement its marketing/publicity. Do not simply depend on your publisher to produce them for you. Unless you have a high-profile (read "high advance") book, your publisher will probably not do more than provide bound galleys for reviewers, flat covers for their distributors and reps and possibly print some postcards, if you ask for them. The rest of the publicity and marketing campaign is really up to you, the author, as are all three campaigns if you are self-publishing.

Did You Know?

Froogle is a free offshoot service from Google.com that focuses on finding products for sale online. You can search for products at <http://froogle.google.com/froogle or list your book for sale at <http://froogle.google.com/froogle/merchants.htm>.

The Materials

Bound galleys are plain-cover, perfect-bound versions of the book that are sent to reviewers early so the reviews can coincide with the book's release and any appropriate blurbs can be included on the back cover.

Postcards and **flyers** carry a picture of the cover plus pertinent sales information: number of pages, physical size of book, ISBN, LCCN, whether a CIP is included, the retail price, contact information for ordering, a brief (postcards) or full (flyers) description of the book and a quote or two. Flyers are used to generate bookseller interest and are especially useful when participating in cooperative mailings, such as through PMA or SPAN. Postcards normally go to potential consumers.

Flat covers are exactly what they sound like: the front, back and spine of the book's paper or dust cover. Distributors and reps carry flat covers, not books, when they call on booksellers.

Book Folios are short, snappy promotional devices used by brokers and agents to sell secondary rights, usually for novels. Usually presented in a three-ring plastic binder with clear sleeves, they contain the following sheets back-to-back:

1) A front cover, including the title of book and author's name, with eye-catching graphics in attention-getting colors that go with the story

2) A one-page synopsis that takes the reader dramatically through the story

3) A single page excerpt of the first chapter

4) A fifty-word pitch that places the book in relation to similar books currently on the market, preferably best-sellers

5) A back cover using the same color scheme, title and author as the front, and includes publisher information and a one-liner on the target audience

Publicists send **press kits** in printed or plain folders to promote reviews and to solicit or arrange author appearances and interviews. They contain:

1) A **one-pager**, which includes the author's photo and short bio, a summary of the book and a few endorsements or quotes

2) A **fact sheet** with a catchy title that lists ten to fifteen brief items that spark interest in the book; the fact sheet for this book, for example, might include statistics or quotes about the book business in general

3) Ten or twelve **sample questions** an interviewer could ask the author to address

4) Two or three **fact-explanation sheets**, that provide greater depth into a few of the above questions or facts

5) The **press release** announcing the book

6) The best two to four print **reviews** or **articles** on the book or author

The **written marketing plan** lays out specifically how you are going to use the above materials to implement the campaign described below.

The Campaign

A marketing campaign that maximizes public exposure while minimizing costs includes **industry mailings, targeted**

advertising, an **internet presence,** and **industry shows,** all enhanced and supported by the author's "dynamic participation," also known as **promotion.**

Industry Mailings

Mailings of various materials can solicit 1) reviews, 2) publicity, 3) representation and 4) sales.

Mailings to solicit reviews must begin several months before the actual release date of the title. Established publishers send out bound galleys to a selected list of important reviewers and/or publications, such as *Publisher's Weekly, Boston Globe, New York Times, Los Angeles Times,* and so forth. Smaller and self-publishers send out flyers or participate in cooperative mailings to lists of independent, local and regional publications/reviewers as well those *crème de la crème,* and forward their bound galleys only upon request. Fair or not, titles from smaller publishing houses and self-publishers seldom capture the more important reviews that the large, traditional houses' titles enjoy.

To solicit publicity in the form of print, broadcast (television and radio) interviews or articles, publicists send out press kits and cover letters directly to the specific editors and producers. Print interviews, which can result in articles about the book, the author or both, are normally conducted over the phone, as are radio interviews. Local, regional, cable and network television interviews or appearances require the author to appear at the appropriate studio. This is the aspect of the marketing campaign that generates the most misunderstandings and hard feelings; authors feel their publishers should be handling it, publishers expect their authors to show up for the few they do schedule, then pick up the ball and run with it for the life of the book. All bestselling self-published titles gained their immense popularity due to authors' constant publicity campaigns.

Established publishers, of course, already have established distribution networks, but self-publishers must solicit distributor and wholesaler representation by supplying a written marketing plan that includes the author's appearance schedule, a press kit heavy on reviews and articles, a bound galley and a flat cover. Small and independent publishers are also required to pay a set-up fee to their wholesalers, and may have difficulty finding a distributor who will take them on unless they make their approach through the PMA programs specifically created for that purpose.

Mailings to solicit sales include flyers or cooperative mailings to booksellers and libraries and postcards to previous consumers.

Targeted Advertising

Dan Poynter, "Mr. Self-Publishing," advocates promotion over advertising, but with the flood of products and books available today, a title needs all the help it can get even if the publisher, bookseller or author has to pay for the exposure. The four forms of advertising are **print**, **broadcast**, **direct marketing** and **web**.

Print

Hundreds if not thousands of books are still sold via half- and full-page **mail-order** ads in newspapers and magazines. Print ads, along with free listings in local papers, are also useful to announce special events such as the book's release, author appearances or special sales.

Soliciting mail orders is direct **Publisher → Consumer** distribution. As with so many other aspects of the book business, there are two schools of thought about mail-order advertising: 1) Once placed, the ad should run consistently and continuously for several issues or 2) since initial response will be the strongest with subsequent appearances attracting fewer and fewer orders, no ad should run more than one or two issues in any given publication. In reality, both the frequency and location of print ads should be tailored to the specific book and marketing plan rather than to generic concepts.

Newspapers and magazines sell two types of advertising: display and classified. Copy for a classified ad can be as simple as a promotional blurb, price and delivery and the contact information for placing an order: address, toll-free number, income-generating number or web address (URL).

Toll-free numbers are paid for by the person or entity advertising the number. Some companies charge a low monthly fee plus all applicable long-distance charges per call; most companies simply charge for the calls at the same rate as if they were outgoing calls. A toll-free number can be directed to ring on any line, so a P.I. service company, the publisher's sales department or even a home phone can pick it up. Toll-free numbers are typically reserved for placing credit-card orders, which generally accounts for a large percentage of any direct-response business. Since plastic is the easiest and certainly most popular payment-of-choice in the 21st Century—a business cannot realistically conduct a direct-sales business without the ability to accept VISA, MasterCard, American Express or Discover Card—a toll-free number is almost mandatory for success.

Income-generating numbers, in the 900 series, are paid for by the calling party. The charges are the applicable long-distance fee plus a usage fee for the call, set by the phone company and its client; usage fees can run any amount of money. Although the client pays a monthly charge for the service, the phone company and client split the usage fee; hence, a 900 (national) or 976 (statewide) line can generate profits even if the product advertised does not. Income-generating lines are customarily answered by a recording, after which the caller can leave a message or an operator can come on the line. They are used to offer additional information about the book or take the caller's name and address to receive an order form or catalog. Today, many people associate 900 and 976 numbers with scams and rip-offs; nevertheless, some small and self-publishers still use them.

Display ads can be double-page, full-page, or part of a page. They can offer income-producing numbers, toll-free numbers, directions to a website and/or clip-and-send coupons for ordering by check or money order. Display ads are most effective when:

- The copy is **long**. Long copy gives the appearance of being an article; people prefer editorial (articles) to ad copy, and tend to read them more closely. To add to the editorial appearance, use a standard typeface and print size.

- Reader **profitability**—the entertainment and/or educational value—is emphasized via testimonial blurbs, review comments, sales figures (illustrating how many other people have enjoyed the book), etc.

- The **headline** is **short**, **punchy**, and **dynamic** enough to draw the reader into the copy.

- Half- or full-page ads are **broken up** with compelling subheads.

- All photographs and/or cover representations are **captioned.**

- An easy-to-use **mail-in coupon** is outlined with the **toll-free number** and **URL** highlighted and repeated in several places.

Broadcast

Television is an especially effective medium for P.I. advertising since it can reach an enormous number of people with a single spot. Time is sold in packages of 10-, 15-, 30- and 60-second spots, with the cost-per-spot varying by station policy, the number of spots in a package and the time of airing. Late night, cable home-buying shows and community or local-announcement stations offer some of the least expensive spots. Response from these ads, however, must be strong enough to offset the expense of filming the broadcast-ready video as well as paying for the package of spots. Infomercials, the talk shows that spend thirty minutes or an hour extolling or demonstrating a product, are most effective when selling how-to, religious, diet, health and business books. Few books are sold on Home Shopping Net or QVS.

Radio advertising, if used at all, should be reserved for advertising events or appearances. The best use of radio is the talk show, which is promotion, not paid advertising.

Direct Marketing

Direct marketing is advertising to consumers whose names have been acquired through mail order or P.I. sales, "rented" from list brokers or acquired via the Internet. To sell effectively through traditional direct mail, send an initial promo sheet or catalog followed by a series of additional mailings. Rented names can only be solicited once; however, when a consumer places an order, his or her name becomes a permanent part of the in-house mailing list. Telemarketing, another option of direct marketing, is handled in a similar fashion, with a script replacing the promotional literature. Calls are made off an in-house customer list or a rented list. Those who buy become part of the in-house list. Few books are pitched via telemarketing, but thousands are sold through direct marketing.

Because postage rates continue to rise, direct mail efforts must be highly focused. Lists should be purged regularly to eliminate expensive dead wood and examined by service bureaus, if necessary, to ensure that all addresses are deliverable. Barcode all mail whether sending with a regular or metered stamp or postal permit. Of the three, the post office handles metered mail first, regular-stamped mail second and permit-imprinted mail last.

In the direct-marketing business, the most important asset a business can possess is customer good will. Liberal return and immediate-ship policies are a must. A **liberal return policy** means the customer can return the book(s) for any reason and get a full check or credit card refund, postage paid—that is, the publisher pays the return postage. An **immediate-ship policy** means the order is shipped within twenty-four to forty-eight hours of being received.

Web

Web advertising includes pop-up ads, associated links from complementary sites, search-engine sponsorship ads and paid positioning on such Internet bookseller sites as Amazon.com, to name a few. No firm rules have yet been created for web advertising; new opportunities arise daily even as old ones disappear into the ethernet. Nonetheless, the "wide-open, everything free" atmosphere that existed during the early days of the World Wide Web have definitely been replaced by more of a business-as-usual, cash-for-services attitude. To make the most effective use of the Internet today requires a combination of paid advertising, strategic alliances, a viable presence and continuous web publicity.

> **Strategic alliances** occur between companies that host each other's links and provide support for each other's products or services.

Viable Internet Presence

Less than a decade ago, authors could get away with claiming they would set up a web site when and if they found a publisher. Today, the Internet is a formidable force in its own right, and no author can expect to reach his public or satisfy his publisher without his own site that provides all the information of a **press kit** as well as **links** to the publisher and/or online booksellers who carry his title. Because the Internet is a notoriously amiable, if not necessarily well-functioning, information source, other book- and writing-oriented sites will also include links to similar sites, provided those links work in both directions. You can list your title and your professional book-writing services on Dan Poynter's, John Kremer's and Writer'sWeekly sites, to name just a few, and via Google, Froogle, Yahoo, Ask Jeeves, and dozens of other search engines. You can also create **strategic alliances** with organizations that complement your subject, book clubs that list your title and reading groups that review similar kinds of books.

In addition to individual websites and online booksellers, the web offers hundreds of "virtual" **book fairs, reviewers** and **discussion groups** that can keep an author's name in front of the Internet public. Many authors post teasers of new and upcoming books on their sites, offer ebooks, host **message boards** and **chat rooms**, maintain **guest books** and provide links to other sites that relate to their books, subjects or readers' interests. Authors can do "live" inter-views, communicate one-on-one with their fans, post their schedules and keep their readers informed of the progress on their next book. Continuous **web publicity** can be outsour-ced to a Web Publicist or PR firm, and would include pitch-ing the book to online **reviewers, newsletters, reading groups, booksellers** and so forth.

Industry Shows

The members of the book industry come together at three kinds of shows: conventions, conferences and trade shows.

Conventions and sales conferences perform the same function, but from opposite ends. The largest international book convention is the Frankfurt Book Fair every October in Frankfurt, Germany. The principal industry convention in this country, BookExpo America (BEA), is staged late spring every year in a major city such as New York, Chicago or Los Angeles. Regional shows, such as the New England Booksellers Association, Upper Midwest Booksellers Association, Northern California Independent Booksellers Association and North Atlantic Independent Booksellers Associations, are all smaller, localized versions of the BEA, which was formerly called the American Booksellers Association (ABA) Exposition. At all bookseller shows, publishers and cooperative marketing organizations such as Publishers Marketing Association (PMA) and Small Press Association of North America (SPAN) display their catalogs to distributors, reps, wholesalers, booksellers and commercial buyers. Sample copies, bound excerpts, P.O.P. displays, catalogs and promotional materials such as buttons, wall posters, shopping bags, elaborate displays, free wine, snacks, candy bars—any and everything is used to entice convention attendees to stop by the booths and review the new frontlists, established backlists and advance titles. Smaller conventions are also held throughout the year by various associations for genre-specific works in such fields as children's, academic and scientific books, among others.

Sales conferences are staged by publishers to introduce their next catalogs' titles to their salesmen or reps. The larger publishers hold their sales conferences in New York, the traditional home of the book industry, but smaller conventions take place all over the country. Publishers can take advantage of their various reps being in one general area by arranging for a meeting place in a hotel or commercial meeting room to announce new strategies, specials and commission and/or bonus incentives. Middlemen represent and promote many publishers' lines; individual salespeople can be motivated to "push" a publisher's line a little harder if they are assured of the company's cooperation and enthusiasm. Financial stimulus, of course, can also be a positive contributing factor.

Trade shows, such as for children's titles or college bookstores, allow a publisher or author to sell directly to the people most likely to buy a title. Carol J. Amato, for example, who wrote and published *The World's Easiest Guide to Using the APA,* among other style-guide manuals, sells tens of thousands of books every year based almost entirely on her attendance at college trade shows.

Author Promotion

(a.k.a. Dynamic Author Participation)

> # Did you Know?
> If you do five things for your book every day, something good will happen. If you do not, nothing will happen.
>
> John Kremer, Editor–in-Chief of *Book Marketing Update* and author of *1001 Ways to Market Your Books*

Where the publicity department is the entity that sets up interviews and articles, the author is the one who has to appear and answer the questions. The marketing department may secure and advertise book signings, but the author is the one who has to show up at the appropriate location, sit behind a card table, sign books, shake hands and keep a smile on her face for two to four hours—before going on to the next appearance. In fact, **author promotion** is all about appearing in public, whether in person, in print, via broadcast or on the web, and is the crux of supporting both the marketing and distribution campaigns to help launch a book, maintain its popularity and ensure its place on the bestseller lists. While the publisher may spend three months promoting a book—"You can expect a hundred review copies and an ad; after that, it's probably up to you." Chris Gavaler, author of *Pretend I'm Not Here* (HarperCollins, 2002)—the author should continue to promote his title until the next one is released.

This may be the hardest part of being an author. Writers are generally far more comfortable communing in solitude with their computers, typewriters or pen and paper, staring out the window while their brains search for exact wording or even doing seemingly endless rewrites and edits than picking up the phone to schedule personal appearances, standing in front of a crowd and speaking about themselves or trying to sound fresh and enthusiastic while answering the same questions over and over for dozens of different interviewers.

But that's what sells books.

Author promotion includes appearances at booksellers and industry shows to do **readings** and **signings**, which promote a title's sale within the store in which they are held or the exhibition at which they are presented. **Print interviews** and **feature stories** promote the title and author more generally, but are most effective when timed to direct readers to those readings and signings. **Talk shows**, **radio interviews** and television **infomercials** can direct readers into local bookstores, or urge them to call the publisher's toll-free number where a sales staff will complete a per-inquiry order. Even better than readings and signings, which are hit-and-miss at best and can be quite disheartening if few people show up, are **mini-seminars** and **presentations**. Authors can sell dozens of books at the back of the room (BOR) following **speeches** at organizations' meetings, professional conferences and conventions or cooperative special events, and nonfiction titles can be parlayed into **full seminars** and

classes for corporations, educational institutions, museums, libraries and the general public.

Book publicists, who used to number in the dozens, now comprise a growing service industry across the country. A publicist will help you book, fulfill and reap the publicity benefits of the above appearances at independent and chain bookstores, conferences, book fairs, trade shows and public or privately staged special events around the country. Beyond those standard events, however, is an entire universe of one-shot and ongoing promotion/marketing possibilities. For example:

- Create a bio blurb about yourself that includes the title of your book, and use it whenever you write a letter, send out a mailing, respond to a survey of any kind or introduce yourself at networking meetings, organizations, parties or even job interviews.

- Send review copies to people in your field but outside your personal circle of influence.

- Hand out free ebook CDs at your place of worship, your local Chamber of Commerce, your workplace and your usual hangouts. Find some new hangouts, and pass out your postcards or CDs there, too.

- Create a short presentation centered around your book and book yourself into professional, business, community groups, local book clubs, schools and charity meetings. Most meet on a monthly basis, and are constantly looking for good speakers.

- Make friends with your local librarian, bookstore manager, editors and columnists and enlist their aid in spreading the word about you and your book.

- Spend time on the web joining clubs and message boards, and use your bio blurb every time you post.

These are just a few suggestions; John Kremer, author of *1001 Ways to Market Your Book*, offers an entire newsletter of ideas every month in his "Book Marketing Update." SPAN's "SPAN Connection" provides monthly marketing and promotion ideas to authors as well as small publishers. Jerrold Jenkins "The Jenkins Group" lists dozens of ways to get your title in front of consumers. It's *your* book—go out and sell it!

Fulfillment

Fulfillment refers to the physical aspects and bookkeeping involved in selling a book: warehousing, shipping and receiving, order taking, invoicing, banking, etc.

Physically, fulfillment means **packing** one or more copies of a book from its shelf in a warehouse into a padded envelope, box or carton; including a **bill of lading** or **packing list**; sealing, addressing, affixing **postage** or completing a **shipping form** and conveying the package to the post office or freight carrier.

The **bookkeeping** aspect involves all of the functions of running a business: keeping track of who ordered what, when, at what price, for what delivery and on what terms. Shipping can either be FOB the warehouse (the buyer pays the shipping) or the buyer's address (the publisher pays the shipping). Sales tax must be applied when applicable, credit cards and checks must be transmitted and approved and invoices, statements and receipts must be generated. Income must be collected, recorded and banked, and all applicable taxes, royalties and commissions must be paid.

Distributors, wholesalers, fulfillment houses and some printers will warehouse, ship, generate the appropriate paperwork and handle the caging, or banking functions, leaving the taxes, royalties and commission functions for the accounting department or independent accounting firm. Statements and checks are generated for reps, co-marketing publishers, distributors and sales taxes on a monthly basis and quarterly or biannually for royalty-paid authors.

Other records publishers customarily keep include mailing lists with each customer's ship-to address, bill-to address, title(s), number per title, price per title, volume discount, customer discount, payment terms, postage/shipping cost and terms, method of original contact and sales history; customer demographics and sales tracking per customer, title, distributor, rep, advertisement, direct mail and promotional event.

On a $19.95 retail book costing $2.49/copy

	Pays	Sells @	Earns
Wholesaler	50% or $9.98	30% or $10.46	$0.48
Distributor	65% or $6.98	30% or $10.46	$3.48
Bookseller	70% or $10.46	Retail or $14.95	$4.49
Publisher	$2.49	Avg. 57.5% or $6.35	$4.48
Author			Avg. 8.5% of wholesale or $0.64

Author Costs — Concept-to-Sales

	You Do It	Someone Else Does it
Writing	$0	$30,000 - $150,000
Submissions	$35 - $75	$1,500 - $8,000
Publishing	$1,500 - $15,000	$100 – 5,000 (Subsidy/Vanity Press)
Distribution Marketing Promotion Sales	$15,000 - $150,000	$500 - $2,500/month

Glossary

ABI Advance Book Information, necessary to list a book in Forthcoming Books in Print and Books in Print.

Access point numbers reference numbers that allow librarians to locate a specific title in the Library of Congress, ISBN system, or any independent cataloging system that supplies its own numbering.

Acquisition editor individual at a royalty publisher or book club that decides if a book meets the company's standards and needs and, if so, arranges to buy the rights from the author.

Action text that conveys 1) physical movement of a character or 2) an entire scene that moves the story forward.

Active voice writing that uses non-passive verbs and/or is unencumbered by superfluous prepositions, articles, gerunds, ambiguities and fallacies.

Adhesive case method of binding. The spine is prepared as in perfect binding, then an endsheet combined with a strip of stretch cloth is applied across the spine. The adhered pages are assembled into a hard case cover.

Adjective word that modifies a noun.

Advances flat payment or series of payments remitted to an author against future royalty earnings.

Adverb word that modifies a verb.

Advertising "U"s Unique, Useful, Urgent and Ultra-Specific

Advertising paid promotion.

Alliteration repetition of initial sounds in adjacent words or syllables.

Anecdote a short narrative, usually funny, that draws a reader in or illustrates a point; the nonfiction equivalent of fictional action.

Assignment book projects developed by packagers, producers or specific-type publishers who hire writers.

Audience who will read a particular book. Also known as target market.

Audio Book spoken version of a book, usually recorded by the author, a celebrity or a professional voice-over artist.

Author credentials previous published work or applicable background that illustrates authority for writing a specific book.

Author intrusion information the focus character either does not know or would not think, feel or believe.

Author that person whose ideas, stories, theories and so forth are the basis of the book, whether or not he actually writes the manuscript.

Background history of a character, assertion or situation. Used to inform the reader of earlier events or circumstances and establish a specific perspective for what happens now.

Backlist titles those still in the publisher's catalog from previous seasons.

Backorder orders that cannot be delivered because a new shipment has not yet arrived from the printer.

Bar codes scannable magnetic lines used to encode ISBNs, prices and zip codes.

Bio author's single-page promotional write-up.

Bluelines copies of stripped negatives before the plates are made, in multiples of eight. Unnecessary with digital printing.

Blurbs 1) a one- or two-sentence description of the book, its appeal and/or its audience (promo blurb), 2) see endorsements (testimonial blurb).

Book design type style, headline placement, page format, artwork placement, etc.

Book doctor a.k.a. **line editor** individual who corrects structural and text flow.

Book folios promotional devices brokers and agents use to sell secondary rights to novels.

Book manufacturers printers with a focus and expertise in printing, assembling and binding books.

Booksellers companies or individuals that buy books at a discount and sell them directly to the consumer.

BOR (Back of the Room) sales generated at seminars, presentations, workshops and so forth.

Bound galleys photocopies of camera-ready pages that have been contained in a temporary or semi-permanent binding.

Burning the plates the process of making aluminum or plastic plates from the stripped negatives for printing.

Camera-ready clean, sharp pages and/or artwork that can be photographed for duplication.

Caricature shallow, one-dimensional, cartoon-type characterization.

Catalog 1) a publisher's books actively being sold, 2) a physical booklet.

CD compact disk.

Character 1) person whose actions and/or personalities are integral to the plot of the story or the flow of the nonfiction narrative; 2) personality traits that distinguish one character from another and makes each interesting.

Character study a pre-writing exercise to determine the character's physical appearance, psychological make-up, economic status, personal, social and business background and so on.

Chart the story plot development technique that employs a column for action offset by a column that defines why the action takes place.

CIP Cataloging in Publication, a reference number that gives librarians a starting point for classifying titles.

Cliché a trite phrase or expression.

Cluster a marketing term for the classification of people according to spending habits, income and interests.

Coherence sentence arrangement that demonstrates the relevance of each detail or idea as well as the logic of its juxtaposition with preceding and succeeding sentences.

Collaboration a joint effort where more than one individual receives copyright and byline credit. Also referred to as co-authorship.

Collaborator one involved in a collaboration, as described above.

Color separation turning colors into a series of cyan, yellow, magenta and black (CYMK) dots.

Co-marketing the practice of buying or holding on consignment a few copies of a selected title for direct marketing.

Commercial buyers schools, libraries, and target markets.

Composition the steps of typesetting and keylining.

Concept a work's topic or fictional theme, audience, book type and category.

Concept initiator person who originates a book project.

Conjunction a word that joins one part of a sentence to another part.

Consistency the flow within and between individual sentences, paragraphs, chapters, etc., achieved by maintaining the same tone, sentence structure, diction, mode of organization and development, and point of view.

Consumers the final buyers.

Convention event in which publishers display their new line to their sales force.

Copy editing an examination of the final text to correct spelling and word usage errors.

Copy editor individual who corrects technical writing errors.

Copyright registration of a work with the Library of Congress.

Cover design the front and back cover of the bound book.

Credits listing of the books you've authored, ghosted and/or edited.

Customer demographics classifying customers.

D.B.A. 1) the abbreviation for "Doing Business As," 2) the public notice necessary when setting up a new business.

Delta binding a method of binding. Cheesecloth is glued to the perfect-bound spine and the cover is glued only to the sides, not to the cheesecloth.

Description narration that tells what a setting, character or object looks like.

Desktop publishing the formatting and printing of camera-ready pages on a personal computer.

Development 1) depth or content, 2) the gradual exposure of facts, character, plot and so on.

Dialogue spoken conversation; i.e., a character speaks aloud.

Digital Publishing production method. All printing is done directly from computer files, not camera-ready printed sheets (hard copy).

Digitizing act of inputting all material—text, illustrations, photographs, internal artwork, cover art and so forth—into computer files.

Direct marketing a method of marketing that encompasses P.I. and direct mail.

Direct mail advertising efforts or literature sent directly to the consumer.

Display marketer a bookseller who buys in large quantity and sells at deep discounts through special events to corporations, hospitals, schools, learning centers and nonprofit organizations.

Distribution the channels through which a book is moved from the printer's or publisher's warehouse to the buying public.

Distributors companies that represent certain publishers on an exclusive basis.

Droit moral "the right of the artist to have his work attributed to him in the form in which he created it." This right does not currently exist in the United States.

Drop-ship the practice of buying copies as orders come in and having the original publisher ship directly to the buyer.

Dust jacket the paper cover that protects a hardcover book.

eBooks inexpensive publishing format that reproduces a book in pixels that can be read on a computer or hand-held Reader.

Editing text revision.

Edition see "revised."

Endorsements or **testimonials** positive comments made by celebrities or people of note who have read the book; also known as blurbs.

ePublishers publishers who produce eBooks.

Exposition explanation or story "telling."

Fact sheet press-kit piece. Ten to fifteen brief items that spark interest in a book.

Fact stuffing inappropriate dialogue technique for providing salient information.

Fact-explanation sheets press-kit pieces. Briefly discuss a specific aspect of a book.

First draft initial, unedited manuscript written without care for grammar, formatting or careful wording.

Flat cover front, back and spine of the paper or dust cover.

Flush cover a cover that has been trimmed the same size as the inside text pages.

Folio page number.

Formality the level of intimacy between author and audience.

Fulfillment physical aspects of selling a book such as warehousing, shipping/receiving, order taking, invoicing and banking.

Function word words such as the, and, a, but, in, to, at, because, while, etc., which express relationships among other words to change sentence meaning.

Gathering the assembling of folded sigs in proper sequence.

Genre fiction writing that conforms to a specific style and format, i.e., mystery, romance, Gothic.

Gerund "ing" verb used as a noun.

Ghostwriter writer who maintains the bylined author's voice during development, writing, rewriting, doctoring and/or copy editing of a book.

Graphic art line art for diagrams, specifications and image reproductions.

Half tone black and white photographs and illustrations other than line art rendered into dots to emulate shades of gray.

Hard copy printed pages.

Hardcover stiff cardboard-covered book; also referred to as cloth-bound, in reference to the outer layer of material.

Hiatus a manuscript space break indicating the passage of time (forward or backward) or a change of location.

Illustration visualization of thought.

Imprint name used by a parent company to indicate the division or subsidiary that publishes the book. Writer's Digest Books, for example, is an imprint of F & W Publications.

Industry mailings letters, flyers, postcards or press kits to solicit reviews, publicity, representation or sales.

Inflection change in word form or voice tone.

Infomercials advertisements disguised as talk shows that spend 30 minutes or an hour extolling a product or book.

Interjection an exclamatory word used to express emotion.

Interviews information gathered first-hand from experts or parties deeply involved in a given field.

Inventory the number of each title in stock.

ISBN International Standard Book Number, an access point number that allows location of a specific title regardless of other similar or identical titles, authors or publishers.

Justification uniform line endings.

Kerning adjusting the space between certain pairs of letters so the text looks better, such as in the word "win."

LCCN Library of Congress Card Number, an access point number that allows location of a specific title regardless of other similar or identical titles, authors or publishers.

Leading amount of space between lines.

Line art any design in black and white without gray shades that does not comprise dots; line art is printed the same as text.

Line editing a sentence-by-sentence examination of the rewritten text to correct interruptions of the flow, grammatical inconsistencies and errors, structural gaps, and stylistic lapses.

Literary agents individuals or companies that arrange deals between authors and publishers.

MEGO (My Eyes Glaze Over) syndrome resulting from trying to absorb too much technical information at one time.

Mail order 1) orders collected by mail from advertising in magazines, newspapers, and so on; 2) orders collected by mail from direct solicitation, also known as direct marketing or direct mail.

Mainstream non-genre fiction that appeals to the general reader.

Manuscript analysis the art of finding the positive aspects in any manuscript.

Market analysis research that details where the book's appeal lies and includes the book's classification by genre or subject, the reader's age/education level, comparable books that have sold well, and so forth.

Market the different outlets, routes, areas, and so forth, in or through which a title can be sold.

Marketing distribution and promotion.

Mass market 1) retail stores that are neither trade nor specialty; 2) paperback books.

Meet in the middle plot-development technique that lays out fifteen scenes by jumping back and forth between the beginning and end of the story.

Middle-men specialty sellers, distributors, reps.

Mood how the action is viewed by the speaker or narrator: indicative, imperative or subjunctive.

Networking method of meeting people and exchanging business cards at organized functions.

New titles those released since the previous catalog, for the current season.

Noun the basis of a sentence that names or classifies someone or something.

Number the singular and plural form of nouns, pronouns, verbs, and so on.

Offset the modern method of printing where a correct-direction plate offsets the printing onto a backwards cylinder that offsets it onto the paper in the correct direction.

Off-the-record not quotable.

One-pager press-kit piece. Summary of the book, author's photo & bio, endorsements or quotes

Out-of-print no longer part of the publisher's catalog.

Outsource to contract other individuals or companies to handle specific functions, such as typesetting, design or fulfillment.

Overhand a cover that is larger in size than the pages it encloses.

Overrun additional printed copies beyond the specified quantity.

P.I. (Per Inquiry) a method of marketing that makes use of a toll free 800 number to take orders.

P.O.D. (Print on Demand) book production method. Pages are produced singly (not in sigs) directly from disk on a high-speed laser printer.

Pacing the speed and proportion of forward movement either of plot or nonfiction exposition.

Packager individual and/or company that coordinates all services and functions necessary for publication prior to sales and order fulfillment. Also referred to as a producer.

Page proofs copies of the designed, typeset, and keylined pages.

Participle a verb used as an adjective.

Perfect binding a method of binding where the sig has been folded and gathered and the edge has been ground off to leave a rough surface. Adhesive and a special lining is applied over the spine (binding edge) before the covers are glued into place.

Person the form of pronoun and verb used to indicate speaker or narrator: first person, second person, and third person.

Perspective the attitude, agenda, thoughts and feelings of the focus character.

Pica a printer's unit of measure which equals approximately 1/6 of an inch. There are six picas to an inch.

Plastic binding a method of binding for books which must lie open and flat where gathered sheets are punched with a series of round or slotted holes on the bind edge and wire or plastic coils are inserted through the holes; also known as spiral or twin loop binding.

Plot what happens in fiction, to whom it happens and how it happens.

Point of purchase display (P.O.P.) table and life-size stand-up poster/racks that hold a limited number of copies of the book.

Point of view (POV) seeing through the eyes of the focus character.

Preposition a connecting word that relates one part of a sentence to another.

Prepress 1) color separation necessary to print color photographs and/or artwork; 2) the progression of steps after editing and before the duplication process: design (typesetting), half-tones, color separations, and page proofs.

Press or news release a general announcement regarding the response to an event, a newsworthy circumstance, or a feature article that highlights the author or book.

Producer see packager.

Professional Book Writer™ (PBW) book-business expert who can consult, critique, author (write), ghost, traditionally ghost, line or copy edit or proofread.

Promo sheet a one-page flyer used to solicit 1) distribution or 2) author appearances.

Promotion the devices used to facilitate distribution and focus public attention.

Pronouns substitutes for nouns.

Proofreader individual who corrects typographical errors.

Proofreading an examination of the final text to correct typographical errors.

Proposal a package used to interest an agent or acquisition editor in a manuscript.

Publicity free promotion or media coverage provided in book and upcoming promotion events.

Publish the functions of prepress through duplication.

Publisher individual or company that pays for the production of a book.

Query letter a request to an agent or publisher for an invitation to submit a manuscript or proposal.

Rag the varying of line endings.

Rasterize to convert vector graphic files into printable bitmap graphic files such as JPEG, GIF, TIFF, PNG, PICT and BMP.

Redundancy repetition of the same point, in slightly different wording.

Reissues books that have been out-of-print and are now reprinted for active sale.

Remainders unsold copies left over after a book has been removed from the catalog.

Repetition operative words repeated within a sentence or paragraph.

Reprint the right to re-release a book under a different publisher's imprint.

Reps companies or individuals who represent a publisher's catalog on a percentage or commission basis but do not carry exclusive contracts.

Resale number the license necessary to pass any sales tax onto the end user rather than the producer.

Retail booksellers trade bookstores, mass markets, and specialty stores.

Returns books sent back to the publisher.

Revised text that has been updated, corrected, or in some way altered. Each revision of a published book is a new edition.

Rhythm the flow or beat of the text that frees the reader from needing to backtrack and re-read, stop and consider, or lose interest.

Rights buyers individuals or companies who purchase specific rights to a book.

Rights clause the clause in a contract or agreement that specifies each party's rights; for collaborative efforts, the clause that spells out how the copyright will be filed and to what extent the writer has editorial control.

Rough draft the initial manuscript before collaborative or client correction, final rewrite, or editing.

Royalties earnings paid to the author, usually based on a percentage of the wholesale selling price.

Royalty publisher a publisher who pays royalties to the author.

Sales advertising and fulfillment.

Sales conference a meeting held by publishers to introduce the line to booksellers and middle-men at large.

Sample questions press-kit piece. Questions that an interviewer could ask an author.

Sans-serif fonts, such as Arial or Helvetica, that do not have small flags on the ends of each letter.

SASE a self-addressed, stamped envelope.

Second printing a second duplication run of a book, using the specific original plates.

Segue fiction transitions for changing time frame, setting or point-of-view.

Self-publisher an author who pays for and/or produces his or her own book. Self publishers derive their income from selling the books they publish.

Serifs the small flags on the ends of each letter. Standard reading fonts, such as Times New Roman or Courier, have serifs.

Setting 1) the specific location of a scene or 2) the time and general area of the book.

Sheet-fed a form of printing that uses sig-sized sheets.

Showing active narration that places the reader in the scene.

Sig or **signature** the sheets that run through the press in multiples of eight.

Slinky flow a logical sequence of information wherein one idea leads naturally to the next.

Slush pile a publisher's backlog of unsolicited manuscripts and proposals.

Smythe sewing the strongest and most durable type of binding, used for hardcovers, where the sigs are individually saddle-stitched and linked to each other by thread; the front and back pages are glued to the insides of the front and back cover.

Softcover a paper-covered book; also referred to as a paperback.

Solicited submission a manuscript or proposal expected by an agent or acquisition editor.

Special artwork illustrations in color or black-and-white that are generated by a non-drawing computer program or an artist in materials other than pen-and-ink.

Special events reasons to buy immediately such as sales, special price reductions, or new shipments.

Specialty sellers or outlets book clubs, brokers, and retail stores that are focused, rather than trade.

Spiral binding see "plastic binding."

Stitched or saddle-stitched binding a method of binding where the sigs have been stapled through the backbone, thus allowing the book to lie flat when opened.

Strategic alliances mutually beneficial associations between companies that host each other's links on the Internet.

Stripping the placement of each negative onto a flat sheet to compose or lay out the sig for platemaking.

Structure the order of paragraphs and sections.

Style a broad term with a variety of applications; attitude is one aspect of style.

Subsidiary right the legal right to print or distribute mass-market editions, reprints, foreign sales, or video, audio or CD ROM versions; to engage in book club or mail order sales; and so forth.

Subsidy/vanity publisher accepts most manuscripts, pays royalties but no advance, expects author to pay all production and marketing costs. Subsidy publishers derive their income from publishing books, not selling them.

Synopsis the story line or how the plot is fulfilled.

Target market who will read a particular book. Also known as audience.

Telling passive narration that explains what is going on rather than letting the reader experience it.

Tense the time an action occurs: present, past, future, present perfect, past perfect, and future perfect.

Third-party voice someone else's written voice.

Titles individual books or manuscripts; not to be confused with copies of the same book or manuscript.

Tracking maintaining records on sales per customer, per title, per rep or distributor, per author, per consumer mailing, and so on.

Trade books intended for the general public or a segment of the general public.

Traditional ghostwriter ghostwriter who researches and writes for celebrities and corporations but does not necessarily maintain the bylined author's voice.

Traditional publisher publishes selected manuscripts after stringent acquisition process, pays advances and royalties, takes all rights and pay for all aspects of prepress, production, distribution and marketing. Traditional publishers derive their income from selling the books they publish.

Transition a composition device that enables the author to change viewpoints or time placement.

Turn-around the practice of using research material to write several articles, an article and a book, or a series of books.

Twin loop binding see "plastic binding."

Typesetting the act of setting the page to appear as specified in the design, allowing for type style, kerning, leading, artwork blanks, and justification.

Unsolicited submission a manuscript or proposal not requested by an agent or acquisition editor.

Vanity press publisher a book manufacturer who offers limited distribution and royalties as part of the paid package.

Verbs words that state, assert, or indicate action.

Virtual publishing fiction or nonfiction posted on the Internet.

Voice the form of verb indicating active or passive action; the grammar, syntax, usage, vocabulary, rhythm and tone of a manuscript that is unique to its author.

Web a form of printing that uses a continuous sheet from a large roll of paper.

Wholesalers companies or individuals who buy from publishers and distributors at a discount, then sell to booksellers and end users at a less-than-retail price.

Work-for-hire an employment circumstance wherein the employer retains copyright, byline credit and artistic control and the writer receives a fee plus employee benefits.

Writer an individual who writes (this distinction which separates the writer from the individual who originates the concept, applies only to the discussions in Section One of this book).

Writer's block common-usage term used to explain lack of inspiration, a condition often correctable by detailing and adhering to an outline.

Links & Resources

Important Addresses

- **Claudia Suzanne**, Professional Book Writer™: Wambtac, 17300 17th Street #J-276, Tustin, CA 92780 (800) 641-3936, http://www.wambtac.com, claudia@wambtac.com

- **R.R. Bowker** (ABI, ISBN, ISSN, Literary Market Place, Books in Print): 121 Chanlon Road, New Providence, NJ 07974 (908) 464-6800, http://www.bowker.com

- **Library of Congress** (Copyright, PCN/LCCN, CIP): Library of Congress, Washington, DC 20059 (202) 707-6372, http://www.loc.gov/

- **Quality Books** (PCIP): 1003 West Pines Road, Oregon, IL 61061 (815) 732-4450, http://www.quality-books.com/qb_pcip.html

- **Dan Poynter**, ParaPublishing: PO Box 2206-224, Santa Barbara, CA 93118 (805) 968-7277, http://www.parapub.com, danpoynter@parapublishing.com

- **Jeff Herman**, Jeff Herman Literary Agency, 332 Bleecker Street, New York, NY 10014 (212-941-0540), http://www.jeffherman.com, jeff@jeffherman.com

- **Jerrold Jenkins**, Jenkins Group, Inc., 400 West Front Street Suite 4A Traverse City, MI 49684 (800) 706-4636, http://www.bookpublishing.com, info@bookpublishing.com

- **Elizabeth Pomada**, Larsen-Pomada Literary Agency, 1029 Jones Street, San Francisco, California 94109,

(415) 673-0939, htttp://www.larsenpomada.com, larsenpoma@aol.com

- **Ellen Reid**, Smarketing, 275 S. Beverly Drive, Suite #100, Beverly Hills, CA 90212, (310) 278-6237, http://www.smarketing.com, ellen@smarketing.com

- **Publishers Marketing Association**, 627 Aviation Way, Manhattan Beach, CA 90266, (310) 372-2732, http://www.pma-online.org, info@pma-online.org

Dictionaries & Thesauruses

- Alternative Dictionaries Collection: http://www.notam02.no/~hcholm/altlang/

- Cambridge Dictionaries Online: http://dictionary.cambridge.org/

- Dictionary.com: http://dictionary.reference.com/

- NetLingo The Internet Dictionary: http://www.netlingo.com/

- Newbury House Online Dictionary: http://nhd.heinle.com/

- YourDictionary.com: http://www.yourdictionary.com/

- Freeality Online Thesaurus: http://www.freeality.com/phrasest.htm

- ROGET'S Thesaurus Search Form: http://humanities.uchicago.edu/forms_unrest/ROGET.html

- Thesaurus.com: http://thesaurus.reference.com/

Grammar & Spelling

- Blue Book of Grammar and Punctuation: http://www.grammarbook.com/

- Grammar Guide: http://webster.commnet.edu/grammar/

- Grammar Slammer: http://englishplus.com/grammar/
- SpellChecker.net: http://www.spellchecker.net/
- SpellCheckit: http://www.spellcheckit.com/
- SpellOnLine: http://www.spellonline.com/

Official Sites

- Library of Congress: http://lcweb.loc.gov/
- U.S. Copyright Office Home Page: http://www.loc.gov/copyright
- Canadian Copyright Licensing Agency: http://www.accesscopyright.ca/

Additional Copyright Information

- 10 Copyright Myths Explained: http://www.templetons.com/brad/copymyths.html
- ABA Copyright Basics: http://www.abanet.org/intelprop/comm106/106copy.html
- Copyright Law: http://www.rbs2.com/copyr.htm
- Stanford University Copyright & Fair Use Articles: http://www-sul.stanford.edu/cpyright.html

Organizations

- African American Online Writers Guild: http://www.Blackwriters.org/
- American Society of Authors and Writers: http://www.amsaw.org/
- American Society of Journalists & Authors: http://www.asja.org/
- American Society of Writers: http://www.
- Black Writers Alliance: http://www.blackwriters.org/

- Canadian Authors Association:
  http://www.canauthors.org/national.html/
- Community Writers Association:
  http://www.communitywriters.org/
- Horror Writers Association: http://www.horror.org/
- International Women's Writing Guild:
  http://www.iwwg.com/
- Mystery Writers of America:
  http://www.mysterywriters.org./
- National Association of Women Writers:
  http://www.naww.org/
- National Writers Association:
  http://www.nationalwriters.org/
- National Writers Union: http://www.nwu.org/
- Novelists, Inc: http://www.ninc.com/
- Poets and Writers Inc: http://www.pw.org/
- Science Fiction and Fantasy Writers of America, Inc.:
  http://www.sfwa.org/
- Sisters In Crime: http://www.sistersincrime.org/
- Society of Children's Book Writers and Illustrators:
  http://www.scbwi.org/
- Writers Guild of America: http://www.wga.org/
- Writers of Color and Culture:
  http://www.writersofcolor.org/

Other Useful Links
- Scribe & Quill: http://www.scribequill.com/
- WriteLinks: http://www.writelinks.com/
- Writers Exchange: http://www.writers-exchange.com/

- Writing-World - Online References: http://www.writing-world.com/links/index.html

Free Online Newsletters

- Book Marketing Update from John Kremer: http://www.bookmarket.com/

- Book Publishing from The Jenkins Group: http://www.bookpublishing.com/

- Bookselling This Week from the American Booksellers Association: http://www.abaflash@bookweb.org/

- Daily Lunch from Publishers' Lunch: http://www.Publisherslunch.com/

- Kirkus Reviews from Kirkus Reviews: http://www.kirkusreviews.com/

- Literary Agents (incl. New Agents Actively Looking): http://www.LiteraryAgents.org/

- Publishing Poynters from Dan Poynter: http://parapublishing.com/

- PW Daily from Publishers' Weekly: https://secure.reviewsnews.com/publishersweekly/subscribe.asp

- PW Religion Bookline : from Publishers' Weekly: https://secure.reviewsnews.com/publishersweekly/subscribe.asp

- The Bookseller (UK) from The Bookseller: http://www.thebookseller.com/

- Writer's Weekly from Writer's Weekly: http://www.writersweekly.com/

Fee-Based Newsletters

- Academic Newswire: from Publishers' Weekly: http://publishersweekly.reviewsnews.com/subscribe.asp

- Publisher's Marketplace:
  http://www.publishersmarketplace.com/
- PW Newsline from Publishers' Weekly:
  http://publishersweekly.reviewsnews.com/subscribe.asp
- PW Rights Alert from Publishers' Weekly
- PW Rights Alert: from Publishers' Weekly:
  http://publishersweekly.reviewsnews.com/subscribe.asp

Registration Sites

- Copyright: http://www.loc.gov/copyright/
- ISBN: http://www.bowker.com/
- LCCN: http://pcn.loc.gov/pcn/
- CIP: http://cip.loc.gov/cip
- P-CIP: http://www.quality-books.com/qb_pcip.html/

Industry Sites

- American Library Association:
  http://www.ala.org/booklist/
- Association of American Publishers (AAP):
  http://www.publishers.org/
- Association of Authors' Representatives:
  http://www.aar-online.org/
- Authorlink: http://www.authorlink.com/
- Booklink: http://www.booklink.com/
- Booktalk: http://www.booktalk.com/
- Bowker Info Site: http://www.bookwire.com/
- Bowker's Free Resources:
  http://www.bowker.com/bowkerweb/resources/free_re
  sources.asp/
- Dan Poynter's ParaPublishing:
  http://www.parapub.com/

- EBook Formats:
  http://www.ebookmall.com/aboutebooks.htm/

- Guide to Writers' Conferences & Workshops:
  http://writing.shawguides.com/

- Jerrold Jenkin's The Jenkins Group:
  http://www.jenkinsgroup.com/

- Media Bistro: http://www.mediabistro.com/

- Media Control Information source
  http://www.inside.com/

- National Writers Union: http://www.nwu.org/

- Northern Lights Publishers' Catalogs:
  http://www.lights.com/publisher/

- Publishers' Marketing Association: http://www.pma-online.org/

- Small Publishers Association of North America (SPAN):
  http://www.spannet.org/

- Small Publishers, Artists, and Writers Network
  (SPAWN): http://www.spawn.org/

- WritersNet: http://www.writers.net

Index

O

P